ALSO BY ROBERT KAGAN

The Ghost at the Feast

*The Jungle Grows Back: America
and Our Imperiled World*

The World America Made

The Return of History and the End of Dreams

*Dangerous Nation: America's Foreign Policy from Its
Earliest Days to the Dawn of the Twentieth Century*

*Of Paradise and Power: America and
Europe in the New World Order*

A Twilight Struggle: American Power and Nicaragua

REBELLION

REBELLION

*How Antiliberalism Is Tearing
America Apart—Again*

Robert Kagan

ALFRED A. KNOPF
NEW YORK
2024

THIS IS A BORZOI BOOK
PUBLISHED BY ALFRED A. KNOPF

Copyright © 2024 by Robert Kagan

www.aaknopf.com

Knopf, Borzoi Books, and the colophon are registered
trademarks of Penguin Random House LLC.

Cataloging-in-Publication Data is available
at the Library of Congress.

ISBN: 978-0-593-53578-3 (hardcover)
ISBN: 978-0-593-53579-0 (ebook)

Jacket image: CSA Images/Getty Images
Jacket design by Ariel Harari

Manufactured in the United States of America
First Edition
1st Printing

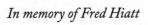

In memory of Fred Hiatt

Contents

REBELLION

Introduction

Virtue will slumber. The wicked will be continually watching: Consequently you will be undone.

—Patrick Henry, Virginia Ratifying Convention, June 9, 1788

T HE INSTITUTIONS THAT America's founders created to safeguard liberal democratic government cannot survive when half the country does not believe in the core principles that undergird the American system of government. The presidential election of 2024, therefore, will not be the usual contest between Republicans and Democrats. It is a referendum on whether the liberal democracy born out of the Revolution should continue. Today, tens of millions of Americans have risen in rebellion against that system. They have embraced Donald Trump as their leader because they believe he can deliver them from what they regard as the liberal oppression of

American politics and society. If he wins, they will support whatever he does, including violating the Constitution to go after his enemies and political opponents, which he has promised to do. If he loses, they will reject the results and refuse to acknowledge the legitimacy of the federal government, just as the South did in 1860. Either way, the American liberal political and social order will fracture, perhaps irrecoverably.

Although this crisis seems unprecedented, the struggle that is tearing the nation apart today is as old as the republic. The American Revolution did not just produce a new system of government dedicated to the protection of the rights of all individuals against government and community, the first of its kind in history. It also produced a reaction against those very liberal principles, by slaveholders and their white supporters, by religious movements, by those many Americans who have sought to preserve ancient, traditional hierarchies of peoples and beliefs against the leveling force of liberalism. This struggle between liberalism and antiliberalism has shaped international politics for the last two centuries and dominates the international scene today. But the same struggle has also been fought within the American system since the time of the Revolution.

The idea that all Americans share a commitment to the nation's founding principles has always been a pleasing myth, or perhaps a noble lie. We prefer to believe we all share the same fundamental goals and only disagree on the means of achieving them. But, in fact, large numbers of Americans have always rejected the founders' claim that all men are created equal, with "unalienable" rights to life, liberty, and the pursuit of happiness, and they have persistently struggled against the imposition of those liberal values on their lives. Great numbers of Americans, from the time of the Revolution onward, have wished to see America in ethnoreligious terms, as fundamentally a white, Protestant nation whose character is an outgrowth of white, Christian, European civilization. Their goal has been to preserve a white, Christian supremacy, contrary to the founders' vision, and they have tolerated the founders' liberalism, and the workings of the democratic system, only when it has not undermined that cause. When it has, they have repeatedly rebelled against it.

A straight line runs from the slaveholding South in the early to mid-nineteenth century to the post-Reconstruction South of the late nineteenth and early twentieth centuries, to the second Ku Klux Klan of the 1920s, to the Dixiecrats of the 1940s and '50s, to Joseph McCarthy and the John Birch Society of the 1950s and '60s, to the burgeoning Christian nationalist movement of recent decades, to the New Right of the Reagan Era, to the Republican Party of today. The issues change— from fluoridated water in the 1960s to vaccines today, from allegedly communist-inspired Girl Scout handbooks in the 1950s to elementary-school curricula today. The circumstances have varied—these movements have arisen in hard times, such as after the 2008 financial crisis, and in good times, in the boom years of the 1920s, the 1950s, and the 1980s and '90s. The media environments have shifted, from newspapers to radio and TV to the internet. But the core complaint has been the same, as is the proposed remedy. All these antiliberal groups—the slaveholding South, the white Southern populists of the Jim Crow era, the Klan, the Birchers, the followers of Pat Buchanan—have feared that their idea of America as a nation of "small government, maximum freedom, and a white, Christian populace" was under attack.[1] All have believed elite cabals involving "Wall Street," Jewish bankers, "cosmopolitans," Eastern intellectuals, foreign interests, and Black people have conspired to keep the common white man down. All have sought to "make America great again," by defending and restoring the old hierarchies and traditions that predated the Revolution.

The most successful leaders of these populist movements have always played to popular fears and resentments of the "elite," the "liberal media," and government bureaucrats who supposedly have contempt for "the people."[2] Like Trump, they have flouted conventional norms of political and social behavior. William Buckley noted that the very "uncouthness" of George Wallace seemed to "account for his general popularity."[3] James Burnham marveled at how Joseph McCarthy's "inept acts and ignorant words" had a "charismatic" quality that well expressed the fears and angers of his devoted followers.[4] Opponents of the late-nineteenth-century white-supremacist populist Senator Ben Tillman of South Carolina called him "a transparent charlatan," recklessly appealing to "the passions and prejudices of the ignorant" and wielding "the dynamic power of hatred."[5] What their critics saw as boorishness and malevolence, however, their followers saw as strength and defiance against a world stacked against them.[6] These were not the tame "conservers" of classical liberalism that some intellectuals claim as the true "conservatism" of America. They have been rebellious opponents of the system, "wreckers," unabashedly antiliberal in both thought and manner, and that is what made them popular.[7]

The Trump movement is no freakish aberration, therefore. Like the demon spirit in a Stephen King novel, it has always been with us, taking different forms over the decades, occupying first one party, then another, sometimes powerfully influential, other times seemingly weak and disappearing. Today it has taken control of the Republican Party as it once controlled the Democratic Party. And although people can point to many recent, proximate causes of its latest manifestation as the Trump movement, the search for such causes misses the point.

The problem is not the design of the American system. It is not the Electoral College, which not so long ago favored the Democratic Party much as it today favors Republicans. It is not political polarization per se, which has often shaped American politics. It is not the internet or Fox News. It is not the economy: these movements have flourished in good times as well as bad. It is not this or that war, or any particular foreign policy. The problem is and has always been the people and their beliefs. As in the past, millions of Americans are rebelling against the constitutional order and the liberalism it protects, and millions more, out of blind political allegiance, fear and hatred of the Democratic Party and "woke" culture, and out of ignorance or indifference to the consequences, are willing to go along with their party's radical antiliberal wing even if it leads to the overthrow of the American system of government and perhaps the dissolution of the nation.

The Radicalism of the American Revolution

The world that is rising into existence is still half encumbered by the remains of the world that is waning into decay; and amid the vast perplexity of human affairs, none can say how much of ancient institutions and former customs will remain, or how much will completely disappear. . . .

—Alexis de Tocqueville, *Democracy in America* (1831)

HOW DID AMERICANS get to this point? To answer that question requires going back to the beginning, to the nature of the American Revolution and the ideas it generated that became the founding principles for the new republic. A liberal tradition was born with the American Revolution, and the radical liberalism of the founding continues to shape and even dominate politics and society in America. But a dissenting tradition was also born, an antiliberal tradition that has done just as much to shape the nation's course, and which is alive and thriving today.

One of liberalism's great weaknesses has always been the belief in its own inevitability. In the liberal mythology, modern American liberalism, and its spread throughout much of the world in the late twentieth century, represented the final triumph of freedom, to which humankind had been aspiring since the dawn of time. It was, in this sense, the "end of history," the inevitable consequence of human beings' desire for autonomy and recognition. From the Renaissance to the Reformation to the Enlightenment, from Magna Carta to the Glorious Revolution to the revolutions in America and France, from Galileo to Newton, from feudalism to capitalism, from agriculture to the industrial revolution. In this Enlightenment teleology, the American Revolution was an inevitable stage in the evolution of humankind.

But the inevitability of liberalism is a liberal myth. From a historical perspective, liberalism, freedom, protection of the rights of the individual have been the rare aberration. Since the dawn of humankind, people have been ruled by tyrannies of one form or another. That is the norm. The predominance of liberalism in the modern world is the exception. It is the product of accident and contingency, of time and place, of wars won and lost. It is due more than anything to the rise of a powerful and all-but-invulnerable liberal power that, like all great powers in history, has shaped the world around it according to its beliefs. Liberalism in Europe in the first half of the twentieth century was on its way out, all but defeated by the powerful antiliberal forces of fascism, until the United States twice intervened to save the liberal world order.

Nor was there anything inevitable about liberalism in America itself. America's liberal Revolution was not the natural outgrowth of "Western" culture, the European Enlightenment, or even the English constitution. It was not the product of an Anglo-Protestant evolution. Its origins are not to be found in Christianity, which, despite its professed belief in the equality of all humans in the eyes of God, nevertheless managed to exist for seventeen centuries without producing a single regime to protect the rights of all individuals equally against the state, church, and community. It grew out of a confluence of unique ideas about the nature of government, a unique interaction of political and international events, and a unique place, North America, where conditions of life, chiefly the millions of acres of fertile and "unused" land for settlement, were different from those in any other place on earth at that time. Like the creation of life, the creation of a liberal republic may not have been a miracle, but it could not have happened without the one-in-a-million concurrence of numerous essential factors. "Western civilization" may have provided some of the key ingredients, but, prior to the American Revolution, Western civilization had produced no liberal regimes. The American Revolution and the founding of the liberal republic were a radical departure, and it is the reaction to that radical liberalism which is the source of today's political and social crisis.

What do we mean by the word "liberalism"? In the latter half of the twentieth century, the word acquired a great deal of baggage: to be "liberal" came to mean favoring a large government role in alleviating poverty, regulating the economy, and providing a whole panoply of social goods; to some it also had implications for foreign policy. To many, liberalism stood for progress, both moral and material. It was a meliorist liberalism in keeping with the Enlightenment's belief in progress and the vital relationship between scientific knowledge and morality, in which the gains in the former invariably translated into gains for the latter. To many, liberalism was synonymous with capitalism and free markets, such that the more free-market-oriented policies of Ronald Reagan and Margaret Thatcher were labeled "neoliberalism" by their critics.

Yet liberalism as it emerged from the American Revolution was both less and more than both supporters and critics often claim. Its sole function was to protect certain fundamental rights of all individuals against the state and the wider community—rights that John Locke identified as life, liberty, and property, with "liberty" encompassing the right to believe in the gods one chooses, or no god at all, without fear of oppression by the state or one's neighbors, and to be secure in one's person from unlawful abuse and seizure. These rights, Locke asserted—and this was what was truly revolutionary—could not be granted by rulers, or even by "the people." They were inherent in the nature of being human—"natural rights," as the American founders called them. The purpose of government—the most important purpose—was to protect those rights. Period. It was not to improve the quality of human existence, except by providing a historically unique form of freedom.

Liberalism is not inherently about progress, therefore, except the progress that comes from the expanding recognition of people's rights. It has no teleology, no final resting point toward which it aims. As Lincoln put it, the principles of natural rights and equality enunciated in the Declaration of Independence were to be "constantly looked to—constantly labored for—and even though never perfectly attained, constantly approximated and therefore constantly spreading and deepening its influence, and augmenting the happiness and value of life to all people of all colors everywhere."[1]

Nor is liberalism itself the final destination on some

journey of human existence, the natural endpoint of some concept of "modernization." Rather, it is a choice, and, at root, a faith. Although its proponents often claim it is the natural product of reason, there is no way to prove that liberal principles are either more "rational" or more "just" than the hierarchical worldview that has guided the vast majority of human beings for almost the entirety of recorded history. Liberalism reflects neither the will of God nor the necessity of history. Either one believes in its principles or one does not.

Nor was liberalism a necessary product of the Enlightenment. The great majority of Enlightenment *philosophes* advocated neither liberalism nor democracy. Their main object was to impose the rule of reason on the world; their main enemy was religion. They believed that nothing could improve the human condition except knowledge, which could only be obtained through rational inquiry, through science. Voltaire worshipped at the shrine of Newton and Bacon and blamed religious "prejudice" and "superstition" for the oppressive ignorance of the masses. He and other *philosophes* "had little concern for the popular masses," however, regarding them as "ignorant, violent, superstitious, and irresponsible."[2] Voltaire had no objection to despotism as long as the ruler acted for the benefit of all by exalting reason over superstition—he was a great fan of France's almost omnipotent king, Louis XIV. Montesquieu admired Britain's "mixed" constitution not because of its democratic elements but because of its separation of powers among the king, the nobility, and the "people" represented in the House of Commons. Rousseau was not a believer in individual rights—the "general will" of the people could be articulated by a benevolent dictator as well as by a popular body. His greatest champion may have been the tyrannical Napoleon. Government, Rousseau believed, had to "force a citizen to be free," and he saw the role of the state as not merely safeguarding the people's interests but seeing to their "moral development."[3]

Whatever the Enlightenment *philosophes* believed, moreover, the world they lived in was moving away from their way of thinking. In the late eighteenth and early nineteenth centuries, a powerful conservative reaction followed the Revolution in France and subsequent Europe-wide war. The Enlightenment's exaltation of reason gave way to blood-and-soil "nationalism" and a deliberately "irrational" romanticism of feeling. Napoleon, the French Revolution's most powerful legacy, made himself emperor and invented the modern police state. The "enlightened" despotisms of Austria, Prussia, and Russia followed his model, using their gendarmeries to seek out and crush movements for liberal reform both at home and abroad. Even in Britain, conservative ministries suspended a number of significant individual rights during and after the Napoleonic Wars in order to ensure the stability of the monarchical and aristocratic regime against pressures for liberal reform and democratization.

A revival of absolute monarchy was fully under way even at the time of the American Revolution. The idea that they lived in a period of democratic revolution and liberal reform would have surprised most Americans in these decades, along with their radical British friends. Neither Thomas Paine nor the more conservative founding fathers like Alexander Hamilton viewed history up to that point as a steady climb to liberalism and democracy. Rather, Paine argued, history "both antient and modern" was a story of the "calamities which have been brought upon mankind" by monarchs in every age, for whose "arbitrary power" "fountains of tears" and "rivers of blood" had been spilled. The present "degenerate age" was even worse, he argued, for by the middle of the eighteenth century the world had witnessed "a greater annihilation of public freedom than seen a century before."[4] In the end, what later historians have celebrated as the "age of the democratic revolution" produced no actual democracies. By the time of Waterloo, the only nation that had democratized at all was the United States.

And what about Great Britain, widely regarded as the most "liberal" of governments in the eighteenth century? The "Glorious Revolution" of 1688 had stripped the king of pretensions to unchecked or "prerogative" powers. In part to justify that king's overthrow, Locke elaborated theories of natural rights that would serve as the basis for the American Revolution and the Constitution, as well as the assertion that governments that abused or failed to protect those rights could legitimately be overthrown. This was the justification for the overthrow of James II in 1688, and for the Americans it would justify independence from George III in 1776.

But for all the power those ideas had in 1688 in England and would achieve in the American colonies in the 1760s and '70s, eighteenth-century Great Britain was not a liberal democracy, nor was it inevitably heading toward becoming one. Parliament wielded sovereign power, and the king was constrained by the terms of that constitutional settlement, but government did not rest on the consent of the governed. As Gordon Wood writes, the English "continued to cling to a medieval conception of society, divided into estates and orders, with the people constituting a single unitary estate alongside the nobility and the Crown."[5] There was a clear distinction and separation between the aristocracy and the common people, with the aristocracy not only enjoying the lion's share of the nation's wealth and occupying the top rungs of society but also enjoying substantial legal and political privileges. For all the liberty enjoyed by Englishmen, in a monarchical society patronage and privilege, starting from the top and cascading down, played a critical role in shaping the lives of citizens.

This much-praised "mixed regime" was not founded on the principle of "natural," universal rights. Insofar as the unwritten British constitution did protect individual rights, they were the rights of Protestants only.[6] The Church of England was at the core of the ruling hierarchy and "operated essentially as a bureaucratic arm of the crown."[7] Throughout the eighteenth and well into the nineteenth century, Catholics could not vote and were excluded from all public offices, subject to punitive taxation, forbidden to possess weapons, and made the targets of official discrimination in education, property rights, and, of course, freedom of conscience.[8] Voting in eighteenth-century Britain was in any case confined to a small minority of property owners, aristocrats, and gentlemen.[9] Elections to the House of Commons involved no more than 15 percent of the total adult male population.[10]

Yet this lack of voting rights did not cause discontent among the great majority of Britons or lead them to question the virtues of the English constitution. Parliament was not meant to speak for the varied interests of the voters. It was an assembly of "one nation," as Edmund Burke put it, "with one interest, that of the whole, where, not local purposes, not local prejudices, ought to guide, but the general good, resulting from the general reason of the whole." As Wood observes, the theory was that "all Englishmen were linked by their heritage, their liberties, and their institutions into a common people that possessed a single transcendent concern."[11] The average British citizen thus "shared the monarchical bias and politically and religiously reactionary leanings characterizing the late eighteenth- and early nineteenth-century British ruling elites and empire."[12]

The monarchy in Britain, meanwhile, was growing stronger, not weaker, as the eighteenth century progressed, largely in response to international circumstances. From the time of the Glorious Revolution to the end of the American war in 1783, Britain fought five major wars, all of them involving the greatest land power on earth at the time, France. The requirements of war and preparedness for war led to the creation of a "fiscal-military state." To fight the wars and manage a growing global empire required a large army and navy at the ready, which in turn required centralization of control, a growing military and financial bureaucracy, and, finally, increased taxes to pay for it all. Taxes increased eight times between 1670 and 1790. By the middle of the eighteenth century, Britain had become "the supreme example in the western world of a State organized for war-making."[13]

The increasing role of the state naturally tended to

strengthen the British Crown, just as it had strengthened monarchy on the Continent. Under the terms of
the 1688 settlement, moreover, the king still appointed
his ministers, and they were responsible to him, not to
the Parliament in which they served. The king and his
chosen ministers exerted influence and produced working majorities in Parliament through bribes and patronage.[14] Yet those who worried about the "corruption" of
the system were in a small minority in England. Average
Britons were content with things as they were, which,
they believed, was how things were always supposed
to be.

From the perspective of North American colonists
across the Atlantic, it all looked very bleak. As one
American summed up the general view in the years
before the Revolution, "Freedom hath been hunted
round the globe. Asia and Africa have long expelled her.
Europe regards her like a stranger, and England hath
given her warning to depart."[15] The Americans were not
joining and advancing an already existing liberal movement when they made their Revolution, therefore. They
were embarking on a new direction of their own.

The World of the Colonies

Circumstances in the British colonies were quite different from those in Europe and Great Britain. Mid-

eighteenth-century colonial North America was probably the freest and most egalitarian place in the world at that time. The main reason was the vast lands available for settlement. The seemingly endless supply of land, often acquired at the expense of the Native American tribes who inhabited it, meant that even those who arrived in the colonies with nothing could, after a period of wage earning, make enough to buy land, become small farmers, and leave behind the wage earner's life forever. This movement from wage laborers, dependent on and necessarily subservient to their employer, to independent farmers was the original "American dream."[16] The rigid class structures that still dominated in Europe and Britain simply did not exist to the same degree in America. A few colonists became rich, and there were enough rags-to-riches stories to make even the destitute in America feel they had a chance to make it. But most became what Thomas Jefferson revered as the common "yeoman" farmer.[17] Neither aristocrats nor gentlemen, these colonists enjoyed a remarkably high standard of living compared with their counterparts in Europe. In England, the wealthiest 10 percent of the population owned a thousand acres of land apiece on average, while 75 percent of landowners held less than fifty acres, and the bottom 50 percent owned less than five acres of land. In the colonies, the average farmer owned fifty-six acres, and these landowners made up 70 percent of the agrarian population.[18] As the French immigrant Michel-Guillaume-Jean de Crèvecoeur put it in his *Letters from an American Farmer*, eighteenth-century North American colonial society was "not composed, as in Europe, of great lords who possess everything, and a herd of people who have nothing." There were "no aristocratical families, no courts, no kings, no bishops, no ecclesiastical dominion, no invisible power giving to the few a very visible one."[19]

The fact of greater equality was accompanied by greater perceptions of equality than existed anywhere in the Old World. There was still deference, a sense that some people were "gentlemen" and some were not. But these distinctions were more visible in the cities than in the areas of new settlement. Since the new tracts of land were in lightly governed frontier settlements, those who managed to survive the hardships did not have to show deference to or seek to win the favor of a court or nobility. Indeed, they greeted with suspicion and hostility any suggestion of social hierarchy. On the frontier, social status didn't matter. Rich and poor alike faced the same hardships, the same challenge of carving a life out of the wilderness. As a leading historian of the American frontier put it, "Men came to accept the idea of equality . . . because as they looked around them, they saw men equal."[20]

The wide and relatively equal distribution of land also had the effect of enfranchising a much larger percentage of the adult male population in the colonies. Whereas in Britain fewer than 15 percent of adult males could vote, in the colonies before the Revolution between 50 and 60 percent of white adult males had the vote. State legislatures, many of which held annual elections, tended to be highly responsive to local demands, in sharp contrast to the House of Commons, which, as Burke argued, was not supposed to be responsive to particular interests but only to the nation's interest as a whole. The colonists thus developed a sense of representation very different from that experienced by most Britons in the mother country. They expected to elect their representatives and to have those representatives respond quickly and favorably to their demands.[21]

The contrast between the New and Old Worlds struck contemporaries on both sides of the Atlantic. As the American poet and diplomat Joel Barlow put it, the social arrangements in Europe accustomed "people to believe in an inequality in the rights of men." It taught them to acknowledge "the birth-right of domineering" and prepared "them for civility and oppression."[22] But in the colonies Burke saw a "fierce spirit of liberty . . . stronger . . . than in any other people of the earth."[23]

There was nothing inevitable about the transformation of the American colonies into a liberal democracy, however. By the 1760s, some in the colonies worried that their natural egalitarianism was giving way to growing aristocratic impulses. Part of the problem stemmed from the colonies' amazing growth. The cumulative "gross national product" of the North American colonies multiplied many times over between 1650 and 1770. Colonists' per-capita income grew at twice the rate in Britain. This unprecedented prosperity over time allowed a few to accumulate great landed fortunes and along with them the desire to emulate the style and manners of the British aristocracy. "The most ancient, settled parts of the province, which are Rhode Island, Connecticut, and the southern part of New Hampshire," as one contemporary observed, contained "considerable landed estates, upon which the owners live in much the style of country gentlemen in England."[24] Fear of the degenerative effects of "luxury" was a staple of Enlightenment thinking, and also of the Puritan heritage, which still influenced many colonists. The accumulation of wealth, it was thought, produced indolence and moral laxity and ultimately decline. Had that not been the undoing of ancient Rome? Moreover, as colonists gained both wealth and social standing, some aspired to positions within the British Empire. George Washington and Benjamin Franklin both sought British imperial postings. Even with wealth, there was only so far a colonist could rise in what was, despite everything, still a social backwater of the empire.

The colonists in these years did not question the

virtues of the English constitution, moreover, and why should they have? The existing system suited their needs, and they enjoyed the rights and privileges that came from being citizens of the British Empire. They sometimes questioned Parliament's decisions, but they did not question the legitimacy of their government, and they did not oppose the king. Despite the special conditions that pertained in the colonies that tended to undermine the authority of London, Wood argues, until the Revolutionary period, "the theoretical underpinnings of their social thought remained largely monarchical."[25]

Toward a New Theory of Government

That way of thinking began to change in the 1760s. At the end of the Seven Years' War, known to the North American colonists as the French and Indian War, the London government was determined to get the empire in order. For decades, British policy toward the colonies had been one of "benign neglect." But when war with France concluded and vast new North American territories were brought into the empire, some rationalization and control seemed overdue. Among other things, the British government sought the colonists' help in paying for a war that, after all, had provided the colonists access to the vast, fertile Ohio River Valley up to the banks of the Mississippi.

London intended both to extract money and to strengthen the governance of the colonies, which meant exerting greater control over colonial behavior. For instance, and much to the fury of the colonists, the British government in 1763 prohibited settlement in a large portion of the newly acquired territory, parceling it off for the Native American tribes with whom the British hoped to maintain peace, and drew the borders of the new province of Quebec to include much of the northern Ohio Valley, which the colonists coveted. These actions showed, among other things, the widening gulf between the interests of the colonists, who wanted free rein to settle where they chose, including on territory recognized by treaty as belonging to the Native Americans, and the government in London, which wanted peace and tranquility following seven years of war, as well as relief from the heavy costs of conflict. Two years later, the government infuriated the colonists again by imposing a tax on all colonial legal and commercial documents, as well as newspapers, pamphlets, and almanacs.

The two measures raised a storm in the colonies, and although London ultimately relaxed or repealed some of the controversial provisions, the actions revealed to the colonists that they were not as free and autonomous as they had imagined during the decades of benign neglect. The Proclamation Line of 1763 and the Stamp Act were both onerous burdens that not only hit the colonists in their pocketbooks but greatly limited their opportunity for growth and individual advancement. Prominent colonists like John Adams saw their career prospects dim in the new arrangement.[26]

Just as troubling to many colonists, London began trying to remodel the colonies along the lines of Britain's hierarchical society. Imperial officials proposed the establishment of an American nobility, appointed by the king, that would eventually become hereditary.[27] This, too, threatened the careers of North Americans, but it also threatened the colonists' freer and more egalitarian society. Many saw these actions as an attempt to subject them to tyranny by a king and a Parliament that no longer defended their rights as Englishmen.[28] For the next dozen years, the colonists would be embroiled in a great debate about the proper relationship between the empire and the colonies, and also about the meaning of representation and the purpose and design of government.

Until then, Americans had not much questioned the virtues of the English constitution. On the contrary, they were mostly under the impression, understandable if mistaken, that the great freedoms they enjoyed and the lack of oppressive hierarchies in their society were, in fact, the product of that constitution, rather than of their unique North American circumstances. When things began to turn sour, therefore, beginning in 1763, they were at first easily convinced by the radical Whig or "country" thinkers and writers in Britain that the danger lay not in the British system of government per se but in its corruption by the king and his ministers. Only over time did they stumble, unwittingly and even unwillingly, toward the conclusion that no arrangement with either the British Parliament or the king could preserve and guarantee their freedoms.

It is easy to dismiss the colonists' expressed fears of becoming "slaves" to the British Empire as an extravagant and disingenuous way of objecting to paying taxes, but the issue went beyond taxation. It concerned the right of Parliament to levy taxes on the colonial economy without the colonists' approval. Representatives elected by constituents in England could not be expected to consider adequately the interests of colonists three thousand miles away. Those members of Parliament were "perfect strangers" as far as the colonists were concerned, and were obviously "not bound by interest, duty, or affection" to protect the colonists' liberties.[29] By setting the Proclamation Line, giving parts of the Ohio Valley to Quebec, and instituting the Stamp Act and other new taxes, Parliament had obviously not considered the colonists' interests ahead of the metropole's. At the end of the day, what the colonists discovered to their horror was that under the existing British system their rights and freedoms were not guaranteed. They were conditional, dependent on the whims of the king and his advisers in London.

Terrible proof of the precariousness of their rights came after the Boston Tea Party in 1773, the culmination of a series of colonial protests centered in Boston to which the British government finally determined to put a stop. In what the colonists came to call the "Intolerable Acts," the British closed the Port of Boston until restitution was made for the destroyed tea; abrogated Massachusetts's charter, reducing it to a crown colony; replaced the elected local council with officials appointed by London; forbade town meetings without prior approval; enhanced the powers of the military governor, General Thomas Gage; and ultimately stationed significant numbers of troops in Boston, forcing inhabitants to quarter the soldiers in their homes.[30] By early 1775, there was one British soldier to every five inhabitants in Boston.[31] In response to the intolerable acts, representatives from all the colonies convened in a Continental Congress in 1774. The first fighting between colonists and British troops occurred at Lexington and Concord in April 1775. The Declaration of Independence came the following year.

The colonists had initially sought something short of independence. They first insisted that the various parts of the empire—the motherland and the colonies—should enjoy equal standing as self-governing entities under the overall rule of the king, in whose person the empire would be united. This would bring the North American colonies out from under the rule of Parliament and make their colonial legislatures supreme and effectively equal to Parliament. Some prominent Britons at the time, including both Burke and Adam Smith, thought London would be wise to agree and grant substantial autonomy to the colonists. Otherwise, they warned, the increasingly powerful colonists might just take it for themselves. "The British Empire must be governed on a plan of freedom," Burke argued, "for it will be governed by no other." But few Britons, least of all George III and his ministers, were prepared to accept this loose definition of their empire. King George rejected the colonists' suggestions and declared his determination to "withstand any attempt to weaken or impair the supreme authority of this legislature [Parliament] over all the dominions of my crown."[32]

George III's rejection of any change in the way the colonies were governed did not only drive the colonists to revolution and independence. It also forced them to come up with a justification for rebellion and, even more important, a new basis for their rights. It was in this search for justification for breaking free of British control that the colonists turned to the very modern but hitherto untested concepts of "natural rights" and the "social compact" propounded by John Locke.

In some respects, this was no great reach. Like all Britons, the American colonists had long believed they possessed inviolable rights. The powerful influence of Locke's ideas of natural rights could be seen in the many pamphlets and sermons of the two decades prior to the Revolution. But until the actual break with England, most colonists had not turned to Locke. They assumed that the rights they demanded, and which had been so brutally violated by the Intolerable Acts, accrued to them through the English constitution. They believed, as Englishmen did, that protection of their rights was part of their contract with the king, a contract that went back to Magna Carta.[33] It was only when it became clear, in their eyes at least, that the king was reneging on that contract that the colonists were compelled to turn to the idea of universal natural rights, not tied to the English constitution. They did so by appealing to the relatively new concepts of a "state of nature" prior to government and of a "social contract" as the basis for government, ideas popularized by the mid-seventeenth-century writings of Thomas Hobbes, and then by Locke. Following Locke, the Declaration of Independence, drafted primarily by Jefferson, stated that if the Crown or the Parliament persistently failed to carry out its primary obligation to protect the people in their lives, liberties, and property, then the people had a right to take back sovereign power and form a new government that could protect them.

The people could, as the Declaration claimed, frame a new government on such principles "as to them shall seem most likely to effect their safety and happiness."

This shift in the basis of the American colonists' rights was subtle but revolutionary. Having begun their protests against London's policies by asserting their rights as Englishmen, the colonists, in breaking away from England, now asserted their "natural rights" as human beings. These rights were not derived from the English constitution or from an ancient compact with the king. They were not the accretion of centuries of English customs and traditions, as Burke and other British political thinkers argued. They were universal rights, enjoyed by all men, regardless of nationality, culture, and history. "The sacred rights of mankind are not to be rummaged for, among old parchments, or musty records," Hamilton wrote. "They are written, as with a sunbeam, in the whole *volume* of human nature, by the hand of the divinity itself; and can never be erased or obscured by mortal power."[34]

This assertion, for it was no more than that, departed from all European and English traditions. From time immemorial, peoples had organized themselves by family, tribe, and, in the modern era, by nations where collectives of tribes were rooted in a common land and linked by common blood, ethnicity, and, usually, religious belief. Few societies in history had ever recognized individual rights at all. Those that did had recognized rights for their own kind, not for others. Even in societies where religions other than the state religion were tolerated, that tolerance was conditional. A ruler could grant it or take it away. Not even the ancient Athenians believed in true freedom of speech or thought, as the trial of Socrates famously illustrated. Ancient republics, even the most democratic, like Athens, placed the needs of the polis above the rights of the individual. It may have been true, as modern liberals have argued, borrowing from the very unliberal Hegel, that all human beings seek "recognition" of their dignity as humans. But although they seek recognition for themselves, their family, their tribe, their co-religionists, their compatriots, few ever acknowledge that others who are not like them—who are of different religions, tribes, and nations—also have an equal right to "recognition." Certainly, eighteenth-century Britons did not believe that other races and religions enjoyed the same rights as Englishmen, or that they should. Nor, as we shall see, did most North American colonists. They were led by unusual and unforeseen circumstances to adopt this radical, universalist ideology.

Jefferson acknowledged as much in the Declaration. The "truths" which he declared to be "self-evident," that all men were "created equal" and were "endowed by their

Creator with certain unalienable Rights," and that "to secure these rights" governments were "instituted among Men, deriving their just powers from the consent of the governed," were not a description of fact. This was a statement of faith, or, as Jefferson and his colleagues saw it, a statement of reason deduced from nature. Locke's philosophy, although it claimed to be based on empirical observation, was on some critical issues based more on Euclidian logic than on observable reality. It was this kind of reasoning—the assertion that certain things were "self-evident"—that informed the Declaration. Jefferson and his colleagues knew that, as a matter of historical fact, no such governments had ever actually been "instituted," that no system had ever actually "secured" those "unalienable Rights" or treated all people as if they were created equal. Jefferson and his colleagues were proclaiming a theory of government, but one on which no actual government had ever been founded. This, they knew, was truly a *novus ordo seclorum,* a "new order of the ages," and it would have massive and revolutionary ramifications for the government and society that the founding generation would establish.

The colonists had not started down this road when they first began protesting against British impositions. Even as late as July 1775, as Jefferson noted, "a separation from Great-Britain and establishment of republican government had never yet entered into any person's mind," and even for much of 1776, "independence, and the establishment of a new form of government, were not even yet the objects of the people at large."[35] They sought only to undo the oppressions exacted by Parliament, not to sever their "contract" with the king. Had George III and his ministers been willing to accommodate the colonists' demands for substantial autonomy, as at least some prominent Britons at the time thought they should, there would have been no need for a Declaration of Independence, no need for separation from the Crown, and therefore no requirement to seek and discover a new basis for the colonists' rights. They could have continued to enjoy their rights as Englishmen, as they had for decades. And though it is impossible to predict the course of development from there, it is not difficult to imagine colonial society continuing on the path it was on in the years prior to the Stamp Act, with the colonials increasingly adopting the social and political norms of the metropole, as most colonial peoples tend to do.[36] Perhaps imperial officials would even have succeeded in establishing in the colonies a hereditary aristocracy of the kind that existed in Britain. That the colonies were destined to achieve some form of autonomy from Great Britain was all but certain—they were growing too large and too rich to remain subordinated to the distant motherland forever. But there was nothing in their behavior up to the early 1760s that anticipated such a radical leap in their theory of government.

This raised an important question: Did the colonists, who had been content with the English constitution as the basis of their rights, really believe in the new, radical concept of universal, "natural rights"? Thomas Paine wanted to believe that, as a result of the Revolution, Americans' "style and manner of thinking" had also "undergone a revolution": "We see with other eyes; we hear with other ears; and think with other thoughts than those we formerly used."[37] But was that really true? A majority of colonists before the Revolution, it is fair to say, did not believe in universal rights, certainly not the slaveholders who dominated the Southern colonies, but not the Northerners, either, whose prejudices against Catholics were almost as great as their prejudices against Black people and Native Americans. The gap between the old traditions and habits of the colonists and the universalist principles of the Revolution was wide at the time of the founding and would grow wider over the course of the nineteenth century. The new, radically liberal tradition in America would from the beginning be accompanied by an antiliberal tradition every bit as potent.

—

This gap was not yet apparent during the height of the confrontation with the British Empire. During the years that began with the Revolution and culminated in the drafting and ratification of the federal Constitution—which is to say, the formative years of the new republic—Americans focused almost exclusively, even obsessively, on securing their "natural rights." Never again would such a high percentage of Americans be so fixated on just that issue. Yet the revolutionary and founding generations, with their unusually intense obsession with their own individual rights, ensured that the question of individual rights and how best to protect them would be the central issue of American politics and society for the rest of the life of the republic. Future generations of Americans would have to grapple continually with the contradictions between the lofty promise and purpose of the founding, and the realities of American society, including the many racial, ethnic, and religious prejudices of its people. But there could be no doubt of the intentions of the revolutionary and founding generations. The system of government they created in this period was first and foremost an individual-rights-protection machine.

The intense focus on rights in this period was understandable. British policies in the 1760s and '70s left Americans with an unusually clear understanding of the specific rights that needed protecting; some of what would be written into the Bill of Rights was a direct response to British actions, especially in Boston after the Tea Party, when freedom of speech and assembly was prohibited, soldiers were quartered in colonists' homes, and any customary rules governing search and seizure were ignored. The Americans, having declared independence and fought a war precisely because their rights had been violated, were not about to establish a new government that failed to protect them from the very same abuses. As one American writer put it, "A bare conquest over our enemy is not enough. . . . Nothing short of a form of government fixed on genuine principles can preserve our liberties inviolate." This, Jefferson said in the spring of 1776, was "the whole object of the present controversy."[38]

Other significant factors contributed to the Americans' obsession with safeguarding their rights. One was the unique circumstance of the founding itself. Unlike the English Revolution of 1688, the American Revolution was not about reforming existing institutions and working out new bargains, or restoring old bargains, between king and people.[39] The Americans had tried to negotiate new arrangements with George III, but when that failed and they declared independence, they entered something approximating the "state of nature," with no king, no state church, no hereditary nobility, and no parliament. As Paine put it in 1776, Americans had "a blank sheet to write upon."[40]

Americans indeed faced an entirely different set of choices from those of the English in their revolution. In England in 1688, the people were trying to take back rights that they believed had been unjustly taken from them by the crown. Americans faced the opposite dilemma. After independence, the people were already in full possession of their rights. The question for them was how much of their rights and autonomy were they willing to part with in order to make a government possible? For many Americans, the answer was: as little as possible. For the drafters of the federal Constitution, the answer was: as little as possible consistent with an effective, functioning government capable of defending itself in an anarchic world.

The question was made even more fraught and complex by the fact that the new government had to be a republic—i.e., without a monarch or an aristocracy. With no monarch or other higher authority to enforce the laws or to adjudicate among competing interests, the people were left both to make and enforce the laws and to adjudicate among their own competing interests. Such a system could function only if the majority of the people accepted the government's authority *voluntarily,* and they would only do so if they believed its powers were sufficiently circumscribed. Taken far enough, this was not a prescription for strong government but for anarchy. Tory critics warned that once the colonists separated themselves from Britain and the Crown, "the bands of society would be dissolved." Hamilton, too, worried that when the people were "loosened from their attachment to ancient establishments" they were apt "to grow giddy" and "more or less to run into anarchy"—which was what happened in France before Napoleon brought a semblance of order through what was essentially a popularly approved tyranny.[41]

The Americans did not quite fall into anarchy, but suspicion of government, any government, became an animating force in American politics and remains so today. This initially took the form of jealous preservation of the rights of the former colonies, now called states, against any form of centralized national government. Most Americans regarded their state as their "country" and naturally looked to their own elected state legislature for defense of their rights, not to any other, more distant body. And, indeed, one of the striking features of the state legislatures as they existed in the period between the Declaration and the ratification of the federal Constitution twelve years later was their extreme responsiveness to the demands of voters. The Articles of Confederation approved by the Continental Congress in November 1777, which governed the republic until ratification of the federal Constitution, ceded practically no power to a central authority. It would take a huge national debate to convince a majority of the states to grant more power to a central, "federal" government, and by no means were all Americans persuaded, even after ratification, that the states had not given up too much.

Even within the states, authority was shaky. Shays' Rebellion in Massachusetts was only one of many such uprisings in the western portions of the states, where frontier and settler families regarded even the state governments as distant and overbearing. Geography, again, determined politics. As first the Puritans, then the British, and now the leaders of the early republic learned, it was not easy to impose anything on people who lived at great distances in undeveloped frontier regions and who always had the option to move elsewhere. Such people were likely to be more jealous of their rights than people in Britain or on the Continent, who were effectively imprisoned by their physical and economic circumstances. And, in fact, every effort to compel obedience of North American settlers, from their first arrival at Jamestown and Plymouth Rock in the early seventeenth century onward, had foundered on the same shoals— namely, the constant availability of land and settlement farther west.

The Americans' circumstances in the first years of the new republic would shape the tenor of American politics and society thereafter, ensuring that the government's authority would always be precarious. This was the Lockean dilemma. If the people had an inherent right to overthrow a government that they deemed systematically unwilling or unable to defend their natural rights, then no government could survive without substantial—and continuing—popular consent. As Jefferson put it, "Our rulers can have authority over such natural rights only as we have submitted to them." If the people voluntarily granted certain powers to a government, they could always take them back if they felt these were being abused. Many Americans, having exercised that prerogative in rebelling against Britain, kept their fingers on the trigger as the new state governments attempted to exert *their* authority.

Indeed, Americans would not even trust a popularly elected legislature to protect their rights. They knew that democratic deliberation alone was not sufficient guarantee against tyranny—it was the British Parliament, after all, the people's body, that had trampled their rights in the 1760s and '70s. As Jefferson warned, "Bodies of men as well as individuals are susceptible to the spirit of tyranny." There was such a thing as an "elective despotism."[42]

This lesson seemed confirmed, some believed, by the behavior of the states during the period of the Articles of Confederation. In the eyes of Madison and other members of the revolutionary elite, the state legislatures exhibited all the dangers of majoritarian democracy. On the one hand, demagogues, "blustering, haughty, licentious, self-seeking men," were gaining "the ear of the people."[43] In addition, various different interests competed for favors and emerged as nascent political "parties," much to the horror of eighteenth-century statesmen who regarded party and "faction" as the bane of democratic government, "the dangerous diseases of civil freedom . . . the first stage of anarchy." The actions of these highly democratic state legislatures raised anew the question of whether too much unconstrained democracy might actually be detrimental to the protection of minority and individual rights. Might not a "popular assembly . . . under the bias of anger, malice, or a thirst for revenge," commit even "more excess" against the rights of the individual than an "arbitrary monarch"?[44]

These elites were especially troubled by economic measures passed in many states—the issuance of depreciated paper currency, the confiscation of property, the suspension of debt collection—which had the deliberate aim of reducing the amount of money debtors had to pay their creditors. It was the triumph of a popular majority over an unpopular, well-off minority of merchants and bankers. To Madison and others, it was clear that the state legislatures were all too responsive to the people's "transient and undigested sentiments," with the result that "interested majorities" trampled "on the rights of minorities and individuals."[45] Worse still, the state assemblies were "drawing all power" into their "impetuous vortex."[46] Washington himself lamented, "We have, probably, had too good an opinion of human nature in forming our confederation." Even if the new government was going to rest entirely on the consent of the governed, something more was needed to protect individual rights. As Madison put it, what was needed was "a republican remedy for the diseases most incident to republican governments."[47]

The remedy was to be found in the written constitution that Madison took the lead in drafting. Here is where the new focus on "natural rights" came into play and created an entirely new theory of government in America. The English constitution had been understood as a contract between the Crown and its subjects, from Magna Carta to the settlement of 1688, a contract that safeguarded the people's traditional rights and freedoms. This distinguished the English from most monarchies on the European Continent, who ruled, they claimed, by divine right, which gave them absolute power. The English idea of a contract between the king and the nobility or the people did make a revolutionary presumption, that both the nobility and the people had rights which the king was bound to respect. But the origin of those rights in the English system was vague and ill-defined. Locke had promulgated the idea at the time of the 1688 Revolution that those rights were "natural" to all humans, but for most Britons, the authority of the king was just as "natural" as the rights of individuals, and it was the contract between king and people that made for the mixed constitution that Enlightenment *philosophes* like Montesquieu found so attractive.

For the Americans, however, the Constitution played an entirely different role. It may still have been a contract between the rulers and the ruled, but in the American case, in a republic, the rulers *were* the ruled. The Constitution, therefore, was really a contract among the people themselves—their "social contract," as Locke called it. Instead of making the legislature supreme—as in Britain, where the Parliament *was* the Constitution, for all intents and purposes—the American system made the Constitution a higher authority that constrained even the popularly elected legislature. A legislature, which governed by the rule of majorities and supermajorities, could not be trusted to look out for the rights of minorities. The Constitution was to be the guarantor of the people's "natural rights," a set of laws that existed prior to and outside of government, establishing the limits of the government's powers, including even that of the "people's" legislature.

The Constitution itself did not "grant" rights to the people, moreover. According to the theory of natural rights, the people already possessed those rights before entering a compact to form a government. What the Constitution did was to "guarantee" those natural rights against any act of the legislature or executive. The Constitution itself, therefore, was not the origin of Americans' rights. It merely codified those preexisting "natural rights" that all humans possessed simply by virtue of having been born human. This unprecedented interpretation of a constitution would have great significance in the future battles over slavery. As Lincoln would later put it, the Constitution was just the framework for the protection and realization of the principles of the Declaration, including the principle of universal individual rights. Employing an analogy from the Bible, he likened the relationship between the Constitution and the Declaration to a picture of a golden apple framed in silver. The Constitution was the silver frame, but the frame was made for the apple, not the apple for the frame. The principles of the Declaration, the belief in the equal and "unalienable" rights of all men, were the true and only essence of the new republic.

Who Is an American? The Founders' View

Later generations of Americans, including our own, have seen in the Revolution and the founding of the republic what they have wanted to see. Both the left and the right, for instance, have tended to downplay the radicalism of the Revolution, even to the point of suggesting it was "conservative"—the left, disapprovingly, because the founders, following Locke, emphasized the inviolability of private property; the right, approvingly, for the same reason, and also to contrast it with the supposedly more radical French Revolution. Millions of Americans have also wanted to believe that the founders set out to create a Christian society, insisting that there was a straight line from the Mayflower Compact to the Declaration of Independence, that both documents grounded the American system, including the rights and freedoms of the people, on a religious foundation.

Yet there is no escaping the clear intent of the founders, which Lincoln recognized. And, indeed, it was on the question of religion that the founders were the most radical. They went out of their way *not* to establish the new republic on a religious foundation and were more successful in this than the supposedly more radical French Revolution—even Napoleon felt the need of a Concordat granting the Catholic Church an official role in French society (when he wasn't persecuting Catholic priests for not accepting his authority over the Pope's).[48] In the new American republic, on the other hand, the various churches were not persecuted, but the role of religion in government was tightly restricted.

There were practical reasons for this. Although a majority of the colonists were Anglican Protestants, this was not the only powerful Christian sect in America. New England and New York were dominated by Calvinists—Presbyterians, Congregationalists, and Dutch Reformed. Baptists and Methodists were on the rise elsewhere, especially in the South. There were also smaller numbers of Quakers, most of them in Pennsylvania, and Catholics, primarily in Maryland, their original colonial refuge. The Anglicans themselves had to separate from the mother church in England and refashion themselves as Episcopalians. The states that had been Anglican before the Revolution had, after independence, disestablished that church.

The problem of multiple Christian sects need not have meant there could be no role for Christianity in general. As Jonathan Israel notes, the founders could have agreed to "an overarching compromise formula of public religion declaring civil power and sovereignty to descend from God, covering main points of doctrine especially belief in the Trinity, and instituting state support and regulation." There was, in fact, considerable popular pressure on them to do so.[49] Yet they did not. Partly this was because some of the smaller Protestant sects feared that Episcopalians would dominate and force their doctrines and practices on those who had come to America precisely to avoid such religious conformity in England. Mostly, however, the founders simply opposed a role for religion in government on principle. Jefferson was blunt: Americans' "civil rights" did not depend "on our religious opinions," any more than they depended "on our opinions in physics or geometry."[50]

The Revolution and the founding of the republic occurred at what may have been the peak moment of Enlightenment thinking on both sides of the Atlantic, a time when the world had been increasingly demystified and scientific explanations were increasingly replacing religious explanations for both natural and human events. Like Voltaire, Jefferson was, at most, a "deist," someone who believed that a supreme being created the universe, established the natural laws that would govern the operation of the universe, but then played no further role. This was God as prime mover, Aristotle's Clockmaker, not the Christian God who created man in His image and sacrificed His son for mankind's sins. The *philosophes'* deity was "nature," or "nature's God." The natural laws established by the creator could be observed and understood by human beings using only their reason. The pursuit of truth was a scientific, not a religious, pursuit. That applied to the understanding of natural rights. They, too, required no theology to discern. Those rights may have been granted by a creator, but they were accessible to man through reason alone. Those "truths" were "self-evident." Nor was it God's task to ensure those rights. That was what humans did in instituting "governments among themselves."[51]

Jefferson's original draft of the Declaration did not make any reference at all to God or any other supreme being but simply stated that all men "are created equal and independent" and that from "that equal creation they derive rights inherent and unalienable." The reference to a "creator" was added later at the insistence of some members of the Continental Congress, and Jefferson probably saw the merit of doing so in a nation in which most people were more conventionally devout than he. But that reference to a "creator" did not make a link with the Puritan founding of Massachusetts Bay Colony. The Mayflower Compact was a statement of the Puritans' godly mission in the New World: to create a devout society in which people could find salvation and be rewarded by eternal life. Unlike the Mayflower Compact, which required godly behavior of all citizens so that all might have a chance at salvation, the Declaration had nothing to do with the afterlife or with godly behavior in this life. It was about the preservation of "natural rights," an entirely worldly task, to be carried out by human beings with no assistance from God, following principles of natural rights that they did not require God in order to comprehend. God is also absent from the federal Constitution. Given another chance to introduce the divinity as a source of Americans' rights, or, indeed, to give it any official role whatever in the governance of American society, Madison and others deliberately did not. It was "we the people" who created the new government, with no reference even to a "creator."

In his *Notes on the State of Virginia,* Jefferson condemned the "religious slavery" that the American colonists, including his fellow Virginians, had been willing to tolerate, even as they "lavished their lives and fortunes for the establishment of their civil freedom." He traced the history of religious persecution in the colonies, from the days of the Puritan settlement, with its harsh penalties for religious infractions, up to the present, when existing English common law, which the Americans after independence never repudiated, still held the death penalty for heresy and many other punishments for various failures of religious observance, at least in theory. Jefferson admitted that in these enlightened times no one was going to be executed for heresy. But would the people always be enlightened? Jefferson was pessimistic. "The spirit of the times may alter, will alter. Our rulers will become corrupt, our people careless. A single zealot may commence persecutor, and better men be his victims." Jefferson warned that there was but a fleeting opportunity to protect that most precious of natural rights: "freedom of conscience."

Many of the founding generation believed religion was an important adjunct for the maintenance of a healthy, virtuous society. Even those hostile to religion, like Jefferson, never sought to eradicate it as the French and Bolshevik revolutionaries did. The founders welcomed religion, but only apart from government. Whatever Jefferson's private views of the universe and "nature's God" may have been, he and his colleagues believed that the intermingling of religion and government had been and always would be the path to tyranny. The issue, for them, was not merely religion but "freedom of conscience," without which, they believed, there could be no freedom at all. The very first amendment to the Constitution spelled out their collective view in the clearest possible terms: "Congress shall make no law respecting an establishment of religion, or prohibiting the free exercise thereof."

Jefferson's pessimism in his *Notes* reflected a general sense that the revolutionary period and early days of the republic were a unique moment, when the American people were most jealous of their rights, most suspicious of authority, most hostile to hierarchies, and most attentive to all the doings of their government and representatives. Jefferson feared that the people could not long sustain this high pitch of concern for their rights. Writing in 1781, two years before the end of the war, he predicted that, once the war ended, "we shall be going down hill." The people would return to their quotidian lives, forgetting their passionate concern for rights, intent only on "making money." They might never again come together "to effect a due respect for their rights," and so their government would stop being solicitous of their rights. This was the moment to set things right, therefore, to establish a sound basis for the protection of rights, whether the citizens continued to demand them or not.[52]

It was not just the question of religion. Jefferson insisted in his *Notes* that "the time for fixing every essential right on a legal basis is while our rulers are honest, and ourselves united." This was the time to remove all "the shackles" on Americans' freedom, for whatever shackles remained "at the conclusion of this war, will remain on us long, will be made heavier and heavier, till our rights shall revive or expire in a convulsion."

In answer to that most fundamental question—who is an American?—the founders were clear that it could be any free person on American soil who was willing to abide by the laws and the Constitution of the United States. American liberalism was not tied to religion, culture, or even race. Free Black people in most Northern states were citizens. Nor was it tied to chronology, privileging those who came first over those who came later. This, too, was partly a reflection of reality. The new American republic was already a nation of immigrants. Although English Protestants made up the majority of settlers in the colonial period, they were hardly alone. The Dutch families who had founded New Amsterdam before it became New York were still dominant in the city and in the farmlands of the Hudson Valley. Swedes had settled in Delaware; French Huguenots had settled throughout the South. Then, in the first half of the eighteenth century, the first waves of German and Scotch-Irish arrived.[53]

Some of the founders did want to limit citizenship to Protestants. Some worried that if the new republic opened its doors too wide, the "discontented of other countries" would "swarm in upon us" in such great numbers that the existing inhabitants would become a "minority in their own country." But the prevailing view was that such immigration (by free white people, of course) was to be welcomed as a constantly renewed source of "Freemen" necessary to populate a society "founded on reason and equality." Jefferson's view was simple: "A foreigner of any nation, not in open war with us, becomes naturalized by removing to the state to reside, and taking an oath of fidelity: and thereupon acquires every right of a native citizen." Any free person could become a citizen who had "resided a certain time" in the country, or whose family members were citizens, or who possessed property—"any or all" of these were sufficient.[54]

The white Anglo-Protestant men who founded the American republic, in short, were perfectly aware that the principles on which they founded it ensured that it would not be a republic of and for white Anglo-

Protestant men only. They were also perfectly aware that this was going to raise difficulties, if not for them, then for future generations of Americans. John Adams predicted, not without trepidation, that "new claims will arise; women will demand a vote; lads from twelve to twenty-one will think their claims not closely attended to; and every man who has not a farthing will demand an equal voice with any other, in all acts of state."[55] Adams did not welcome this, but he knew it was the logical and perhaps even necessary consequence of the moral and political system rooted in the principle of universal individual rights, which he supported. The founders created not only a rights-protection machine but, in declaring the rights of all people, a rights-recognition machine as well. The founders anticipated that groups of people whose rights were not recognized in American society at the time of the Revolution would claim those rights as the liberal ideals of American society took hold.

Slavery and the American Constitution: The "Vicious Bargain"

The new theory of government had massive implications for the pervasive system of human bondage that played a critical role in the American economy, both in the Southern colonies, which depended on slave labor, and in the Northeastern colonies, which depended on the carrying trade in Southern staple products that slave labor produced—in the early years rice, indigo, and tobacco, and then, increasingly, cotton. In the decade following the Declaration and through the drafting and ratifying of the Constitution, everyone engaged in the debates over the formation of the new republic knew that the continuing existence of slavery contradicted the very principles of universal natural rights on which the entire nation was to be founded. In raising the banner for universal natural rights in their dispute with Great Britain, the revolutionary colonists had struck a blow against all manner of privileges and hierarchies, and that included slavery, whether they all liked it or not.

The American Revolution produced the first serious abolitionist movements on both sides of the Atlantic.[56] There had been no such movement to speak of prior to the Revolution, and although the first abolitionist movements with any clout were led by North American and British Quakers and evangelical Protestants in Britain like William Wilberforce, the roots of abolitionism were not primarily religious. As proslavery advocates never tired of pointing out, the Bible treated slavery as part of the natural order of things—as a product of divine will—and both Catholics and Protestants had for centuries regarded keeping other men and women in bondage as perfectly consistent with a Christian life. The Anglo-Protestant tradition may have produced Lockean theory, but as a practical matter its much greater contribution lay in one of the most brutal and most racially grounded forms of slavery known to history.[57]

The practice of slavery did not end with the Revolution, needless to say, but the traditional justification for it became problematic. Those who could most easily afford to abandon it did. During the Revolution and the period of the Articles of Confederation, numerous states passed legislation abolishing slavery either immediately or gradually. Massachusetts, in its 1780 constitution, declared all people born "free and equal," which the courts interpreted as abolishing slavery. Pennsylvania's Gradual Abolition Act of 1780 noted that slavery "deprived" Black people "of the common Blessings that they were by nature entitled to."[58] By 1804, every Northern state had either abolished slavery or put it on the road to extinction. Even in the South, some slaveholders freed their slaves in response to the new "revolutionary ideology."[59] As Gordon Wood observes, the "ideas" that the former colonists developed in their controversy with England—ideas of human equality, which even Southern slaveholders endorsed, in theory—were immediately "turned against themselves."[60] Northern critics of slavery were quick to condemn the glaring contradiction. As one leading Quaker abolitionist put it in 1783, now that they had declared to the world that "all men are born equal" and were "equally entitled to liberty" according to "immutable laws of nature," it was necessary to "demonstrate your faith by your works" by promoting "equal and impartial liberty to all those whose lots are cast within the reach of influence."[61]

No one more completely embodied the great contradiction of the Revolution and the founding than Jefferson. The author of the Declaration and its ringing assertion of the equal and "unalienable" rights of all men had no doubt in his own mind that these principles applied to Black people. Neither Jefferson nor, at the time, even the leading Southern slaveholders denied that Black men were men. Jefferson also did not deny that, because of the institution of slavery in North America, half of the population was able to "trample on the rights" of the other half. Indeed, not only was Jefferson fully aware of the moral injustice of slavery, but he even invoked the God he barely believed in to condemn it. Confident that "God is just" and that "his justice cannot sleep forever," Jefferson "tremble[d]" for the future of the country.

At the same time, Jefferson himself was a racist in every sense of the word. He believed Black people were genetically inferior. In his *Notes on the State of Virginia,* he spends a good deal of time enumerating what he regarded as their inferior qualities, in appearance, in habit, in intelligence. Jefferson's titanic hypocrisy was well noted at the time. Hamilton observed sardonically that those "who talk most about liberty and equality" held "the bill of rights in one hand and a whip for affrighted slaves in the other."[62] Jefferson was indeed the "owner" of hundreds of enslaved people at Monticello and did not emancipate them while he was alive or make provisions for their emancipation after he died, as Washington did. His wealth depended on forced labor, and he would not give up his plantation owner's lifestyle either for himself or for his progeny.

Jefferson did not minimize the evil effects of slavery, however, including on the slaveholders themselves. On the contrary, he acknowledged what soon became a common Northern antislavery argument: that slavery had a terrible effect not only on those enslaved but also on the moral character of those who practiced it, and not only their moral character as people but as citizens in what was supposed to be a liberal republic. The relationship between master and slave was one of "unremitting despotism on the one part, and degrading submissions on the other." By allowing "one half the citizens thus to trample on the rights of the other," slavery turned the first half into "despots" and the other into "enemies."[63]

Not surprisingly, given this clash between what he openly acknowledged was a terrible evil, on the one hand, and his own selfish interests and those of other slaveholders, on the other hand, Jefferson preferred to put his faith in a miracle—namely, that slavery would eventually end, either through some future legislation or by natural causes. He may not have been willing to give up his own slaves, even after his death, but he was willing that others should eventually be forced to give up theirs. He claimed to favor a proposed emancipation law for Virginia that would have freed all enslaved people born after passage, paid for their education, supplied them with arms and the means of supporting themselves, and shipped them off to "such place as the circumstances of the time should render most proper"—i.e., not North America.[64] Whatever the virtues or demerits of the idea, such legislation never passed in Virginia or anywhere else in the South.

Nor could it have. While some slaveholders, moved by the liberal spirit of the Revolution, did free their slaves, either immediately or, like Washington, after their death, the great majority of slaveholders never had any thought of relinquishing the sole source of their wealth and social standing, or of risking the wrath of those whom they had brutally oppressed for so long.

They also knew, however, that the liberal spirit of the Revolution and the founding of the new republic on radical liberal principles posed a threat to their traditional way of life. They knew that their existence as masters of enslaved people would be under constant threat in the new federal government in a way it had never been before. The very openness of the new democracy ensured that, at least in the North, opponents of slavery could appeal to their elected representatives, who would feel some obligation to take heed of their complaints. As John C. Calhoun observed years later, "A large portion of the Northern States believed slavery to be a sin, and would consider it an obligation of conscience to abolish it if they should feel themselves in any degree responsible for its continuance." Pressures would begin with "the fanatical portion of society," the abolitionists, who would work on indoctrinating "the ignorant, the weak, the young, and the thoughtless," and eventually this movement would become strong enough to obtain political control, at which point those at the top would, however reluctantly, be compelled to "yield to their doctrines."[65] The new state constitutions in the North, moreover, contained no racial restrictions on voting, and so, as the emancipation provisions kicked in, there would be an ever-growing number of free Black voters. Even North Carolina allowed all free men to vote, and that included the state's small free Black population.[66]

Finally, it was clear that, in the new nation, free states were going to outnumber slave states. By joining the Union, therefore, the slave states would be moving from a situation in which no outside power had any say over their slave "property"—except the still-proslavery British government—to one in which they would be forever entangled and potentially pressured by fellow states in the North that had no economic interest in the preservation of slavery and were morally opposed to it.

Knowing that the new federal government was going to be stacked against them, the slave states insisted as the indispensable condition for joining it that the Constitution contain provisions guaranteeing that this new government would never be able to take away their slaves.[67] To compensate for the Northern states' larger populations, Southern representatives demanded that slaves be counted for the purposes of apportioning each state's representation in the House. And although there was some opposition in the North, and some Northern politicians suggested it might be better if the North and the South went their separate ways, in the end the prospect of not having the Southern states join the new nation was almost unanimously regarded as unacceptable, even by Northern antislavery advocates. Could two such nations coexist side by side? Would they not both, in this divided condition, become ripe targets for attack or abuse by some foreign power? These arguments were barely mentioned in the debates over the Constitution, because they were so obvious. The Southern slaveholders also enjoyed some significant Northern support, particularly among the Northeastern merchants who made their living shipping Southern crops, produced by slaves, to Britain and other European markets.

The new federal Constitution drafted in 1787 and

coming into force in 1789, therefore, contained a mammoth contradiction. It was designed to create a liberal political order in which universal natural rights could be most securely protected. Yet it also included special protections for the most antiliberal practice in the world: slavery. This contradiction in effect created two distinct Americas, one predominantly liberal, and one determinedly and necessarily antiliberal. It was not that one part of the country was racist and the other wasn't. Racist beliefs were rampant everywhere, and remnants of slavery even persisted in some Northern states, like Indiana and Illinois. But because the Northern economy was not dependent on slavery, and, in fact, most Northern capitalists and workers alike regarded slavery as inimical to their interests (unlike Northeastern merchants), Northern abolitionists had freedom to speak and organize, and Northern antislavery politicians could be and were elected to office. Thanks to the freedoms guaranteed by the Constitution, pressure from Northern liberals was sure to affect the South.

Anticipating this, the South's representatives demanded that the new Constitution contain guarantees for the institution of slavery. In deference to Northern sensitivities, and also to hide the obvious contradiction, the words "slave" and "slavery" don't appear in the Constitution. But there could be no doubt that the very document that Madison and others hoped would entrench liberalism in America forever, contained provisions that were blatantly antiliberal and that actually doomed the whole liberal project. The three-fifths clause, which counted enslaved people as part of the Southern states' populations for the purposes of apportioning representatives in the federal Congress, gave the slaveholding states a distinct boost in power relative to the non-slaveholding states. This was deliberate. Not only did it ensure that the slave states would not be hopelessly outnumbered by the non-slave states in Congress. It also ensured that the slave states would wield disproportionate influence in electing the president. The Electoral College, though established for other purposes, was also a compromise between the slave and non-slave states that granted the former a representation greater than their voting population alone warranted.[68] With those two provisions, the South hoped to ensure that the federal government would never be controlled by potentially hostile Northern interests, even if, as was already the case, the Northern states were both more numerous and more populous.

In order to provide the guarantees that Southern slaveholders demanded, the Constitution implicitly accentuated states' rights and established an important precedent that has echoed through the nation's history ever since. The general suspicion of strong government that shaped the contours of the new republic became entangled with the slaveholders' demands to limit the federal government's ability to intrude in their affairs. Henceforth, slaveholders and white supremacists of all stripes would appeal to this libertarian founding spirit, which paradoxically both protected American liberalism against a too-powerful government but also, perversely, offered protections for the antiliberal institution of slavery. As Charles Cotesworth Pinckney informed the South Carolina Legislature, "We have a security that the general government can never emancipate them, for no such authority is granted."[69] Whether or not this was true as a theoretical matter—among the purposes of the Constitution, after all, was to address the problem of state legislatures' trampling individual rights—it was undoubtedly the practical reality. In fact, the party controlled by the "slave power," as Northern antislavery politicians called it, managed to hold the White House for forty-four years out of the sixty years between 1801 and the outbreak of the Civil War. Every northern president in this period was either favorable to slavery or indifferent but, in any case, took no steps against it. Such was the effect of the Constitution's various proslavery clauses. It was not until 1860 that a Northern antislavery party was able to put its nominee in the White House, at which point the South seceded.

Some anti-Federalist opponents of the Constitution argued that the union of North and South could never work, that it was "impossible for one code of laws to suit Georgia and Massachusetts." Such a monstrosity, they warned, ran "contrary to the whole experience of mankind," and therefore could only be held together by "military coercion."[70] Like many of the anti-Federalists' warnings, this was prophetic.

2

The Antiliberal Tradition
in America

We are not a free people; we have not been since
the war. . . . If we were free, instead of having negro
suffrage we would have negro slavery. Instead of
having the United States government we would have
the Confederate States government. . . .

—George Tillman, South Carolina
Constitutional Convention, September 1895

THIS WAS THE great disjunction produced by the
American founding. Americans may have changed
their views concerning what made a government legitimate. The oppressions of the British Empire may have
made them acutely conscious and jealous of what they
now called their universal natural rights. But they were
still the same people they had been before circumstances
drove them to adopt this new theory of government. For
the great majority of Americans there had been no lessening of racial, religious, or ethnic prejudice, no rethink-

ing of the role of women, no gradual abandonment of religious traditions. The new liberal order was grafted onto what was in many respects a preliberal and even antiliberal society. As Benjamin Rush put it, "We have changed our forms of government, but it remains yet to effect a revolution in our principles, opinions and manners so as to accommodate them to the forms of government we have adopted."[1]

Scholars have written about the "liberal tradition in America," but there has also been an antiliberal tradition in America, a powerful and persistent dissenting view that emerged at the very beginning and would shape the course of American history for the next two centuries, right up until our own time.

The core and beating heart of this dissenting, antiliberal tradition was the slaveholding South. Slaveholders were not just Americans who happened to own slaves. Nor were they Democrats who just happened to be petty tyrants in their personal lives. They did take part in the system and were willing to engage in the tussle of democratic politics, up to a point. But they were fundamentally and openly antiliberal. They regarded the very idea of universal equal rights as a sham, an absurdity that was contradicted, they insisted, by all of human history. They believed in democracy up to a point, but only if it was an exclusively white democracy, if it allowed them to pursue their antiliberal beliefs and interests, if it controlled others who might critique their way of life, and, above all, if the power of the government was used to help them hold on to their human "property" and not in any way limit their right or ability to hold it. On these terms, they were willing to support the new American democracy, but on no others. Their antiliberalism trumped whatever beliefs about democracy they shared with the rest of the country. When democracy and electoral politics turned against them in 1860, they simply left. It may have been true that the South "in its secret heart always carried a powerful and uneasy sense of the essential rightness" of the antislavery critique, that it "shared in these moral notions" with the rest of the revolutionary generation.[2] But that sense did not stop Southerners from turning fundamentally against the American liberal system established by the Revolution. Indeed, as humans often do when confronted with a clash between interest and principle, it was the principle they jettisoned.

It turned out that even the carefully constructed Constitution, which Southerners thought would guarantee the "security" of their "property" in perpetuity, did not provide all the protection they needed. It did not, for instance, protect them from the effect of large demographic shifts among both white and Black people over the first eight decades of the new republic.

One problem was the predictable advantage in population that the North had enjoyed at the time of the founding, which only grew with the passing decades. It had been precisely to negate that advantage that Southerners had insisted on the three-fifths clause, to compensate for the smaller number of free white voters in the South. But the gap between the Northern and Southern populations nevertheless continued to grow. The comparatively open, industrializing North offered more plentiful and more attractive opportunities for people seeking a better life than the more provincial South, where Black slaves did the great bulk of the work—so much so that the migration of white Southerners to the North was three times greater than the flow in the opposite direction. Meanwhile, of the millions of overseas immigrants who began settling in the United States in the 1830s and '40s, fully seven-eighths settled in the North. The census of 1850 revealed that, in the 1840s alone, the North's population growth exceeded the South's by 20 percent.

The disparity in the growth of the two sections threatened to upset the fine balance created in the original constitutional compact. Even with the three-fifths clause, the growth of the North's population, as well as the inevitable creation of free states in the northern parts of the Louisiana Territory, would over time give the North exactly the control of the federal government that

the South had worked to prevent. As the South Carolina politician James Hammond put it, the North would
"ride over us roughshod" in Congress, "proclaim freedom
or something equivalent to it to our slaves and reduce
us to the condition of Haiti." Southern security lay in
"equality of power," Hammond warned, and if the South
did not act, it would "consign . . . our children to the
flames."[3] That meant expansion, and as the territories of
the Louisiana Purchase began to meet the qualifications
for statehood, the South wanted to ensure that any new
states would preserve the balance.

More unexpected, but just as unsettling, was the
dramatic rise in the numbers of enslaved Black people.
Contrary to the hopes and expectations of people like
Jefferson, the end of the slave trade in 1808, for which
the Constitution had made provision, did not lead to
the reduction of the slave population. The number of
enslaved Black people rose by 70 percent to one million between 1790 and 1810, and by 1860 the number
had soared to three million, the result of surprisingly
high birthrates. Also unexpectedly, the value of slaves
rose considerably in this period. The invention of the
cotton gin in the 1790s drove up the demand for slaves
to work in the cotton fields that proliferated across the
South, including in the territories of the Louisiana
Purchase west of the Mississippi. In 1790, the United
States produced just 3,000 bales of cotton a year. By

1810, annual production had risen to 178,000 bales, and would rise to more than 4 million bales a year by the eve of the Civil War.[4]

The great rise in the slave population strengthened the economic viability of the system but also raised problems for the South. Slaveholders and their non-slaveholding white neighbors began to feel anxious about being trapped and outnumbered. In the words of one South Carolina politician, they were increasingly "smothered and overwhelmed . . . pent in and walled around on exhausted soil—in the midst of a people" bent on "revolt and murder."[5] The solution was western expansion, a "safety valve" to relieve the supposedly dangerous pressures of the swelling Black population. Increasingly, the prevailing view among Southerners was: expand or die.

Unfortunately for the South, the admission of new states, slave or not, required congressional approval. When the Territory of Missouri applied for statehood as a slave state in 1818, the reaction in the North revealed deep hostility to any expansion of slavery. With little warning, a New York Democratic congressman, James Tallmadge Jr., offered amendments to the statehood legislation barring the "further introduction" of slavery into Missouri and freeing all slaves born in the state after its admission once they turned twenty-five. Much to everyone's surprise, including Tallmadge himself, the House approved the antislavery amendments by solid majorities.

The nation plunged into crisis as both sides realized the implications. As John Quincy Adams, then secretary of state, wrote in his diary, the Tallmadge amendment "disclosed a secret," that there was a powerful and widespread animosity in the North to the "Southern domination which has swayed the Union for the last twenty years," and which many in the North were no longer willing to tolerate.[6]

The original bargain was falling apart on both sides. The South, more dependent than ever on slavery, no longer felt sufficiently protected by the Constitution and sought to reestablish slavery on a firmer footing within the system in light of all the demographic, economic, and technological changes that were occurring. Unfortunately, Southerners needed Northern acquiescence to accomplish this. But most of the North, outside of those groups that directly benefited from slavery, was not interested. If anything, the North had turned even more hostile to the slaveholding South since the founding of the republic.

Beyond the obvious differences in the two regions' economies, the ideological and spiritual gap between North and South was also growing. At the time of the Revolution and the early republic, most Northerners and Southerners believed they occupied the same moral universe—the men of Massachusetts and New York joined with the men of Virginia as both revolutionaries and framers. But once the pact was made, the two regions headed off in opposite directions: the North, increasingly shorn of slavery, was liberalizing, industrializing, urbanizing, reforming, democratizing, and, as many would have it, "modernizing," with all the attendant benefits and costs; the South was becoming more deeply committed to slavery as a way of life, and therefore tried to preserve the traditional hierarchies and the beliefs that sustained them, resistant to change and reform, increasingly conservative in the antiliberal sense of the word. Even the religions of North and South diverged, shaped by underlying interests and ideologies. In the North, a surge of religious revivalism began in the late eighteenth century and continued well into the nineteenth—a "Great Awakening"—which, inspired by secular liberal principles, stirred up movements for women's rights, education reform, prison reform, temperance reform, and, most incendiary of all, abolitionism. These reform movements often drew from the same pool of Northern liberals— prominent abolitionists like Charles Grandison Finney, Frederick Douglass, and Theodore Parker also promoted women's rights at a time when that cause was even less popular than abolition. In the South, Protestant evangelical ministers defended slavery, hierarchy, and religious and social orthodoxy. Northerners like John Quincy Adams spoke constantly of progress and believed that the "progressive improvement in the condition of man" was "apparently the purpose of a superintending Providence." In the South, leaders like South Carolina's Hammond damned progress and asked, "Where will all this end?" Where the Southerners feared it would end was with a Northern attack on slavery.[7]

These deep divisions had already opened between North and South when the question of Missouri erupted. The Tallmadge amendment passed in the House but ran into a Southern brick wall in the Senate. Southern political leaders warned that if Congress refused to take in Missouri as a slave state, it would be the end of the Union. Talk of possible secession and civil conflict filled the air. Senator Thomas Cobb of Georgia warned that the amendment had "kindled a fire which all the waters of the ocean cannot put out, which seas of blood can only extinguish." To which Tallmadge and other Northerners responded with equal defiance. "If a dissolution of the Union must take place," Tallmadge thundered, "if civil war, which gentlemen so much threaten, must come, I can only say, let it come. . . ."[8]

The seventy-seven-year-old Thomas Jefferson had lived long enough to see the disaster he had feared play out before his eyes. The Missouri crisis, "this momentous question, like a fire bell in the night, awakened and filled me with terror. I considered it at once as the knell of the

Union." He was not alone. Many observers feared secession and conflict, but many, too, believed there was no
avoiding it. As Jefferson put it, the "North-South geographical line, coinciding with a marked principle, moral
and political, once conceived and held up to the angry
passions of men, will never be obliterated; and every new
irritation will mark it deeper and deeper."[9] John Quincy
Adams also anticipated civil war, but did not shy away
from the implications. As "calamitous and desolating" as
such a war would be, he wrote, if the result was the end
of slavery he could not help but wish for it.[10]

The crisis was temporarily averted by a compromise,
engineered by Kentucky's Henry Clay, which allowed
Missouri to enter as a slave state, with Maine to enter as
a free state, and designated latitude 36°30' as the future
dividing line: above it new states would be free, and below
it new states could enter as slave states. Supporters of
the Tallmadge amendment like New Hampshire's Representative William Plumer Jr. observed bitterly that
the Southerners had "threatened so loudly, and predicted such dreadful consequences . . . that they fairly
frightened our weak-minded members into an abandonment of this most important & salutary measure."[11]
Other compromises would follow, as every new territory
acquired and new state admitted produced new threats
of secession and war. As Jefferson foresaw, each new irritation drove the sections further and further from each

other, until the two national parties fractured into their regional components.

Northern abolitionists played a critical role in keeping the pressure on the South. They were unpopular in both regions and were often charged with a fanatical disregard for the well-being of the country. Nor were their antiracist views and desire to help Black people escape from bondage welcome in what remained a racist society. The vast majority of Northerners did not care what happened in the South, and some of the arguments for "free soil" were just as racist as the South's arguments for slavery: Northern workers did not want to have to compete with slave labor, but white Northerners also did not want Black people flooding into their states.

Yet the abolitionists made progress nevertheless, in part by provoking the South into taking actions that outraged even Northerners who were indifferent to the plight of Black people. The demands of the Southern slaveholders for new slave territory in the West and South brought the issue back to first principles and reminded people of what John Quincy Adams called that "dishonorable compromise with slavery" in the Constitution, a "bargain between freedom and slavery" that was "morally vicious" and "inconsistent with the principles upon which alone our revolution can be justified." He looked to the Declaration of Independence as the true wellspring of American freedom and predicted that it would be "the precipice into which the slaveholding planters of this country sooner or later must fall."[12]

As Northerners increasingly appealed to the principles of the Declaration and saw the Constitution's compromise with slavery as a morally vicious bargain, Southerners responded by repudiating the Declaration altogether. The Virginia politician and slaveowner John Randolph of Roanoke called the Declaration "a most pernicious falsehood." South Carolina's John C. Calhoun called the very idea of equal rights a "false doctrine" that had unfortunately been "inserted" in the Declaration of Independence "without any necessity." In the years before the Civil War, Southern politicians and intellectuals increasingly expounded a straightforward antiliberal doctrine. The social theorist George Fitzhugh argued that the United States was founded on false "abstractions," that "life and liberty" were not, in fact, "unalienable." They had been "sold in all countries, and in all ages, and must be sold so long as human nature lasts." It was the North, he insisted, not the South, that was out of step with the broad sweep of human history. The "peculiar institution" was not slavery; it was liberalism.[13]

The slaveholders and their spokesmen were not alone in adopting this increasingly antiliberal stance. In 1820, only a quarter of Southern households "owned" and enslaved Black people. But white solidarity trumped the vast disparities of the Southern economy and society. As the Southern journalist W. J. Cash explained, the "common white" was no less loyal to the South and its institutions than the rich plantation owner. The reason was race. Non-slaveholding white people were just as "determined to keep the black man in chains" as the slaveholders and saw Northern antislavery agitation as just as much a danger to them.[14] Slavery depended on an acceptance of racial hierarchy, but slaveholders were hardly the only ones who were prepared to fight and die for white supremacy.

In response to Northern pressures, the South circled the wagons. Every criticism of the South was treated as an act of disloyalty, and every critic "stood an excellent chance of being mobbed." In the thirteen years prior to the Civil War, five editors of the leading Vicksburg newspaper were murdered for their views.[15] The state of Georgia officially posted a reward of five thousand dollars to anyone who would kidnap the abolitionist leader William Lloyd Garrison and bring him to trial in the South for inciting Black insurrection.[16]

The need to control the discourse extended well beyond the issue of slavery. Any opening wedge of liberalism was deemed threatening; any criticism of the Southern way of life, resting as it did on the foundation of slavery, was intolerable. As Fitzhugh put it, "If ever the abolitionists succeed in thoroughly imbuing the world with their doctrines and opinions, all religion, all government, all order, will be slowly but surely subverted and destroyed."[17] Already, women at abolitionist meetings were "unsex[ing]" themselves by pouring out "false and foul execrations against slavery and the Bible." It was all of a piece—"slavery, marriage, religion" were the "pillars" of human society, and they were all threatened by the same liberal ideals that produced abolitionism.[18] As one mid-nineteenth-century Southern Presbyterian leader put it, "The parties in this conflict are not merely abolitionists and slaveholders—they are atheists, socialists, communists, red republicans, jacobins, on the one side, and the friends of order and regulated freedom on the other."[19]

Equally threatening to Southern leaders was the growing power and reach of the federal government. The war with Great Britain between 1812 and 1814 produced, as the Revolutionary War had, demands for greater government spending and involvement in strengthening the nation. Even under the Southern leadership of Madison, Monroe, and John C. Calhoun, a growing sense of "nationalism" accompanied new federal programs. In 1824, when John Quincy Adams became the first Northern president since his father's election almost three decades earlier, he brought an ambitious program of federal spending on national projects—building canals and making other improvements in internal transport and communication; proposing federal funding for scientific observatories and explorations; increasing the U.S. role in the hemisphere by sending delegates to a conference in Panama.

Following the Missouri crisis, however, the South opposed any expansion of federal power. It was already intolerable that the South had been forced to accept Congress's right to "interfere and to legislate on the subject" of slavery, which violated the cardinal Southern principle that "the institution of slavery should not be dealt with from outside the South."[20] The South henceforth opposed any expansion of federal power for any reason—even the building of canals. As North Carolina's Senator Nathaniel Macon put it, if Congress could "make canals," it could just as easily "emancipate."[21] Southerners now declared the whole idea of "national" power suspect—as one South Carolina senator complained, the term "national" was "a new word that had crept into our political vocabulary . . . a term unknown to the origin and theory of our Government."[22]

The original tradition of suspicion of government now became entangled with Southern white strategies for keeping Black people under their control. What would later become the American conservatives' fixation on "small government" was inextricably tied up, first, with the protection of slavery, and then, after the Civil

War, with the South's efforts to preserve white supremacy. The South demanded "strict construction" of the Constitution, a kind of "originalism" that focused on the language of the Constitution, which protected slavery, against the liberals' appeal to the Declaration and the "spirit" of the Revolution, which tended to undermine slavery.

Although Clay and others worked to contain the burgeoning conflict through compromise, to buy time for what they still hoped would be the eventual end of slavery, the fundamental clash of ideologies could not be contained. The differences between North and South only sharpened and deepened. In response to the constant attacks from Northern abolitionists in the form of petitions to Congress and abolitionist literature sent by mail into Southern states, the South in the 1830s pushed through Congress a "gag rule" which required that abolitionist literature sent by mail to the South be confiscated at the Mason-Dixon Line and that antislavery petitions sent to Congress be blocked from consideration. As the North became a haven for runaway slaves, Southern slaveholders demanded the enforcement of fugitive-slave laws requiring the federal government and Northern citizens to aid in the return of Southern "property."

The South became increasingly despotic, and not

only toward slaves and free Black people. Preserving the Southern master's authority over his slaves required control of white behavior, too. In the Deep South, white people deemed hostile to the slave regime were lynched. Antislavery agitators, when they were not hanged, were tortured, tarred and feathered, and driven from Southern towns. Kentucky's antislavery politician James Birney was forcibly expelled from the South and became a living martyr to the antislavery cause as well as the North's first antislavery presidential candidate.

The increasing violence in the South strengthened the hand of those in the North who insisted the Union could not continue with slavery. As William W. Freehling notes, "When issues changed from black slavery to white republicanism, from an unfortunate institution on the other section's turf to unacceptable ultimatums about a common democratic government, Yankees stiffened into anti-southern postures."[23] For a twenty-nine-year-old Abraham Lincoln, it raised questions as to whether the nation could survive at all. In an 1838 political address in his home state of Illinois, he cited the examples of a mixed-race man captured by a St. Louis mob and burned to death; the summary hanging of large numbers of Black and white people in Mississippi, sparked by fears of insurrection; and, just a few months earlier, the sensational murder of the abolitionist Elijah Lovejoy by a proslavery mob in St. Louis. Contemporaries later recalled that the murder produced "a burst of indignation" in the North that had not been seen since the Battle of Lexington.[24] Such widespread violence, Lincoln warned, such disregard for the laws of the nation, could only lead to the breakdown of government, which would cease to enjoy the "attachment of the people."

Indeed, just as Jefferson had warned in 1781, Lincoln lamented that the original spirit of the Revolution had dissipated with time, leaving Americans with only the normal selfishness of all human beings. In those early years of crisis and excitement, "the jealousy, envy, and avarice" that were part of human nature were "smothered and rendered inactive," and the "deep-rooted principles of hate, and the powerful motive of revenge" were directed exclusively at Britain. But that heightened state in which the Declaration had been promulgated was fading in people's memories. The original "pillars of the temple of liberty" had "crumbled away." It was left to the present generation to replace them with new pillars.[25]

There was still no consensus in the North for going after slavery where it already existed. No one denied that the Constitution permitted it, and some Northern interests still benefited from the South's posture. Among these were Martin Van Buren and others who founded the new Democratic Party, which, although it enjoyed support in the North, including in Van Buren's home state of New York, nevertheless clearly and openly served

Southern slaveholders' interests. Van Buren promised a national political party that would "be responsive to the South" and would "maintain its identity in relation to the opposition as a states' rights–strict construction party."[26] Thus, the antiliberal South now controlled a national party dedicated to the preservation of slavery.

Even many Northern Democrats continued to draw the line at the expansion of slavery, however. As Lincoln put it, "Toleration by necessity where it exists, with unyielding hostility to the spread of it."[27] This was not as passive as it sounded. Containment, it was widely assumed in both North and South, would spell the end of slavery in the South as Southerners, denied their "safety valve," suffocated in their own hellish prison. "Slavery has within it the seeds of its own destruction," insisted David Wilmot, the author of another amendment to prevent the spread of slavery into territories acquired from Mexico by war in 1848. "Keep it within given limits . . . and in time it will wear itself out."[28] Southerners agreed.

Nor was the North going to be entirely passive. The abolitionists would continue promulgating their doctrines, and the North was not going to silence them. As one antislavery politician from Ohio put it, the North would "establish a cordon of free states" and "light up the fires of liberty on every side" until the chains of slavery were melted and the enslaved Black people set free. This was how the South saw it, too. Ultimately, it was not any

direct intrusion by the North in the South's affairs but
the North's refusal to countenance the further spread of
slavery that produced the Civil War.

Nevertheless, the issue at the core of the dispute was
liberalism. The South argued for a democratic majori-
tarianism within the states while demanding its "rights"
as a slaveholding minority within the nation as a whole.
As the Illinois senator Stephen Douglas argued in his
famous debates with Lincoln, the people of each state
should be allowed to determine whether or not they
would allow slavery without interference from the federal government. What he called "popular sovereignty,"
however, was precisely the democratic tyranny that the
revolutionary generation had feared and sought to prevent. Douglas's insistence that "the people" could vote to
approve the enslavement of others, and that this "democratic" decision to do so gave slavery legitimacy, was a
profoundly antiliberal argument. The founders and the
revolutionary generation had well understood that even
"the people" could be tyrants, and that the protection of
"natural rights" would sometimes require overruling the
decisions of the majority. The nation was founded not on
the principle of "popular sovereignty" but on the belief
that all individuals possessed natural rights that could
not be abridged even by democratic processes. Lincoln
rejected Douglas's claim and called on Americans to
rededicate themselves to the radical liberal conviction

that "all men are created equal," a moral truth that could not be overridden by a mere vote of the people.

Southern leaders pointed out after the outbreak of the Civil War that they were not the "revolutionists" but were "resisting revolution." And they were right. They were resisting the American Revolution. Lincoln was reviving the radical liberal principles of 1776, precisely the principles that the South had always opposed in order to preserve ancient traditions of slavery and white supremacy. As the president of the new Southern Confederacy, Jefferson Davis, correctly observed, "We are not engaged in a quixotic fight for the rights of men. Our struggle is for inherited rights. . . . We are conservative."[29] That was the critical distinction. Black people, of course, had no "inherited rights," and the very idea of "inherited rights" was English and European and rooted American rights in white Anglo-Protestant tradition and culture. At the highest level of abstraction, this was what the Civil War was about, and both sides understood it.

George Washington had foreseen from the beginning that the struggle between liberalism and antiliberalism had to be settled if the Union was to survive. And it could only be settled in one way. "Nothing but the rooting out of slavery," he had warned, could "perpetuate the existence of the union, by consolidating it in a common bond of principle."[30]

3

The Triumph of Antiliberalism

A s it turned out, however, a "common bond of principle" was exactly what the Civil War did not produce. The antiliberal South was defeated militarily and occupied for years by the Union army. Its leadership was decapitated. Its slaveholders lost their plantations. Pushed through by superior Northern political and military power, the Thirteenth, Fourteenth, and Fifteenth Amendments banned slavery, eliminated the three-fifths clause in the Constitution, and acknowledged the right of all citizens to vote, regardless of "race, color, or previous condition of servitude." Questions about whether the Bill of Rights applied to the states and could be enforced by the federal government were resolved in keeping with the original idea that natural rights existed prior to the Constitution and did not flow from the Constitution. The Constitution itself was for the most part "re-purified."[1]

But even though the South was militarily defeated

and deprived of its special advantages in the Constitution, its hostility to liberalism did not abate. The Radical Republicans who controlled Congress knew that, left to themselves, Southern political leaders would do everything possible to restore both slavery (in modified form) and white supremacy. As Massachusetts's Representative Benjamin Butler warned, white Southerners had not yet learned "the lessons" of equality and had to be prevented from returning to "their old ways" and trampling "the rights of freedmen."[2] The "Radical" Republicans, so-called by their opponents, attempted to do this but were stymied both by Southern resistance and by Northern unwillingness to expend the resources and energy that would be required to transform the South sufficiently to make it reliably liberal. This, combined with the indifference, at best, of most Northerners to the plight of the formerly enslaved Black people, practically ensured that the South would emerge with white supremacy intact.

As W. J. Cash observed in 1941, if the war had "smashed the southern world," it had nevertheless "left the essential southern mind and will . . . entirely unshaken," and Southerners themselves determined "to hold fast to their own, to maintain their divergences, to remain what they had been and were."[3] As they regained control of Southern state governments, they immediately set about restoring slavery in all but name, through widespread violence and the murder of both Black and white people, through new laws depriving Black people of the right to vote, and through corruptions of the legal system that produced widespread incarceration of Black people, relegating them to prison and chain gangs. In 1866, veterans of the Confederate army, led by General Nathan Bedford Forrest, created the Ku Klux Klan to murder and terrorize the newly freed Black people and their white supporters. In theory, the North might have compelled the South for as long as it took, but in reality, there was not the will to do so, nor perhaps even the capacity; as Cash suggests, "There were not bayonets enough to guard all the cabins scattered through this wide land."[4]

Nor did the defeat and removal of the elite slaveholder class diminish their influence in the South or the tendency of all white Southerners, regardless of class, to line up with them against Northern liberalism. Indeed, "it was the common white," according to Cash, "and particularly the poor white properly so-called—in whom the Yankee's activities generated the greatest terror and rage, in whom race obsession and passion for getting the Negro safely bound again in his old place were most fully developed."[5] The "common whites" were more concerned with their status vis-à-vis the freed Black people in their midst than they were about economics or class, more interested in preserving a world in which "a white man, any white man, was in some sense a master," and ensuring such a world in perpetuity, so that their sons and grandsons and all their posterity would continue to enjoy this "great heritage of white men."[6]

This determination would not flag for the next century and more, and it is unclear if it has ever flagged, even after a second armed intrusion by the North, during the civil rights era of the 1950s and '60s. Here again, the common assumption about the inevitability of liberalism has led to constant underestimation of the power of antiliberal sentiments in America. We simply assume that, with time, people become enlightened. Yet the views of white Southerners did not change: not in the 1870s, when they fought against Black equality; not in the 1920s, when the second Klan spread across the South like wildfire; not in the 1960s, when George Wallace spoke for millions when he declared "segregation now, segregation tomorrow, segregation forever." And not today, when the unwarranted killing of Black people by police inspires for so many white Americans more sympathy for the police than for their victims.

The fact was, by forcibly bringing the South back into the Union after the Civil War, the forces of liberalism allowed a second major compromise with the forces of antiliberalism. Just as it had been a fantasy to believe that slavery would die off naturally, it turned out it was equally fantastic to believe that the antiliberal tradition in America would die once slavery was outlawed.

Southern white people never accepted the equal rights of Black people, despite the North's impositions.[7]

Restoring the Union not only ensured a continuation of the vibrant antiliberal tradition in America, it also gave antiliberalism a continuing foothold within the constitutional system, even as "purified" by the Civil War amendments. The Democratic Party, which had been captured by the slaveholders in the antebellum years, remained the party of the South, and therefore of institutionalized racism, after the war and for the next century, even under progressive liberal reforming presidents like Woodrow Wilson and Franklin D. Roosevelt.[8]

In the battle against the North and its liberal impositions, control of the Democratic Party gave the forces of antiliberalism the ability to operate both inside and outside the constitutional order. They enjoyed all the power and prerogatives of a party within the Constitution: They could block legislation unfavorable to their interests in preserving white supremacy, using legitimate congressional measures; they could run candidates in free and fair Northern elections, ensuring a voice and a restraint on more radical liberal Northern ambitions; the Democrats in Congress could and did refuse to appropriate money to fund federal troops in the South. They could even occasionally elect presidents, as they did, arguably in 1876, and unquestionably in 1884, 1892, and 1912.

Yet, at the same time, the party, and the white supremacist interests that controlled it, also benefited from
extra-constitutional assaults on liberalism—the widespread violence and brutality directed chiefly at Black
people, but also at white people; the manipulation and
corruption of Southern election results through both
violence and fraud; the enforced unanimity of opinion
in the South, which included violent assaults on journalists, editors, and other critics of Southern society. These
efforts to protect white supremacy also worked to ensure
the Democratic Party's supremacy throughout the South
and were thus tolerated if not welcomed by Northern
Democrats for the national power it gave them. These
corrupt, illegal, and violent means were regarded by white
Southerners as justified and even glorified as a continuation of the fight that had been temporarily lost
in the Civil War. Ben Tillman, the "populist" leader in
South Carolina who served as governor from 1890 to
1894 and then in the U.S. Senate until his death in 1918,
never denied that he and his paramilitary group, the
Red Shirts, gained power "through force and fraud"
and, indeed, openly proclaimed, "White men would
always violently resist attacks on their power."[9] This was
how Southern white people defined their "freedom."
If Southern white people were truly "free," Tillman's
brother argued, "instead of having negro suffrage, we
would have negro slavery."[10]

The antiliberal tradition lived on, therefore, and maintained a firm hold on the crucial levers of the federal government, and not only on matters of race. On matters of religion, too, the traditional ways long survived the attempt by Jefferson and the founders to separate religion from government.

Religion was another area where the liberal principles of the Revolution and the early republic did not match the actual feelings and behavior of much of the American population. Neither at the time of the Revolution nor later did most Americans, regardless of region, share Jefferson's and Madison's view that God had nothing to do with the founding of the republic and would not be taking part in the protection of people's "unalienable" rights. Many if not most Americans saw God's hand in everything, past, present, and future—and, of course, it was their own God they had in mind. Despite the separation of church and state explicitly called for in the Constitution, most of the state governments retained Protestant religious tests for public office for decades after the Revolution. The new Massachusetts postrevolutionary constitution required "all who take seats in the House of Representatives or Senate" to declare their "firm persuasion of the Christian religion," an oath designed to exclude atheists, agnostics, deists, and Jews. That provision remained in force until 1820. New Jersey specifically required state officeholders to be "Protestants"; the South Carolina constitution proclaimed the "Christian Protestant religion" to be "the established religion of this state." New Hampshire effectively debarred non-Protestant officeholders until 1877.[11]

For most of the first century after the Revolution, the main victims of the continuing dominance of Protestantism in American politics were Catholics. Indeed, if Southern slavery and white racism posed the most profound challenge to the new liberal ideals of the American government, virulent anti-Catholicism was a close second. For most Americans outside the South, Catholics were the number-one enemy.[12] Even during the Revolutionary War, John Jay, coauthor of the *Federalist Papers,* first chief justice of the Supreme Court, antislavery founder of the New York Manumission Society, and the descendant of Huguenot refugees, was so passionately anti-Catholic that he tried to insert a prohibition against Catholics' holding office in the New York state constitution and, for the country as a whole, "a wall of brass . . . for the exclusion of Catholics."[13]

Even if the United States did not have an official established church, hostility toward Catholicism, the only religion of any significance in America other than Protestantism, had much the same effect. De facto if not always de jure, the Protestant majority determined which religious practices in the United States were acceptable and could be supported by the government and which were to be penalized. This fundamental antiliberalism thrived throughout the early and mid-nineteenth centuries, alongside the antiliberal bastion of the slaveholding South, and it continued well into the second half of the twentieth century.

To be sure, some of the attacks on Catholics came from liberals. Catholicism, they argued, which theoretically required unquestioning allegiance to the Pope, was inherently hostile to liberty. This charge against Catholicism as antiliberal and antidemocratic would remain conventional wisdom in American academic circles, not to mention the public at large, until deep into the second half of the twentieth century. In the nineteenth century, there was a kernel of truth in it, inasmuch as many Catholics in antebellum America shared with the Southern slaveholders an uneasiness about liberal individualism. Since Catholics had been among the chief victims of the French Revolution, they naturally harbored deep hostility toward the liberal ideals that allegedly informed it. Father J. W. Cummings spoke for many Catholics when he denounced as nonsense the idea that "all men are born free."[14]

As for slavery, the Catholic Church had never regarded it as contrary to God's will, any more than Protestant churches had—England and Holland were both

Protestant nations with extensive overseas slave empires. Only as a result of the American Revolution had a significant number of non-slaveholding Protestants in the North turned against slavery. Yet most Catholics, even in the North, did not make the same journey. All the major Protestant denominations in the mid-nineteenth century had important antislavery wings, but the Catholics did not.[15] Abolitionists like Elijah Lovejoy were anti-Catholic, therefore, and the anti-immigrant Know-Nothing movements of the 1840s and '50s were filled with antislavery advocates who saw Catholic proslavery sympathies as an attack on American liberty. The ranks of anti-Catholics also rose in the 1840s, as liberal refugees from the revolutionary turmoil of Europe led the charge against the "anti-republican, anti-democratic, highly dangerous Roman Hierarchy."[16] In 1861, *The New York Times* defined both popery and slavery as "incompatible with the spirit of the age [and] liberty and civilization."[17] The fact that Catholics seemed aligned with Southern slaveholders made them targets for the principled and for the bigoted.

Nor was there any shortage of ethnic bigotry to complement the religious. The number of Catholics in America grew enormously because of the waves of Irish and German immigrants in the 1830s. The changing complexion of Catholicism mattered. In 1790, there were only twenty-five thousand Catholics in America, most of them French; by 1860, there were 3.5 million, the majority of them Irish.[18] As Roger Daniels observes, "The Roman Catholic church had become an immigrant church."[19] The Irish Catholic immigrants who fled famine and oppression in the British Isles were generally regarded as subhuman, and not white, by much of the native white American population. As Irish immigrants came to dominate the Catholic Church in America, the hostility of the vast majority of American Protestants only deepened.

The increasing democratization of the United States during the early nineteenth century, culminating in the populist presidency of Andrew Jackson in the 1830s, proved no antidote to this bigotry. The greater representation of the white common man did nothing to loosen the grip of white supremacy or diminish the attacks on non-Protestant religions. On the contrary, as more and more white males acquired the vote and popular sentiment played a bigger role in politics, racial, ethnic, and religious bigotry only intensified.

In the 1840s, some 1.7 million immigrants came to America; in the following decade, the number reached over 2.5 million, at a time when the total population of the United States was only a little over 25 million. In 1850, Americans born overseas made up just under 10 percent of the population; by 1890, it would be close to 15 percent.[20] Of the great wave of immigrants in the 1840s, the Irish made up almost half.[21] In Boston in 1850, 35 percent of the population was foreign-born, and of these three-quarters were born in Ireland.[22] Then, between 1850 and 1920, some 30 million more immigrants arrived on American soil.

The first and most obvious reaction to this massive immigration was an intensification of nativism, white supremacy, and Protestant hegemony. The first significant anti–Irish Catholic violence erupted in Boston in 1834, when a Protestant mob burned down the Ursuline Convent outside the city, and more than a dozen churches were set ablaze in the mid-1850s. In New York City, mobs attacked the Church of St. Peter and St. Paul. Everywhere, priests were beaten up.[23] As early as the 1830s, nativist organizations cropped up to oppose letting immigrants vote or hold office and denounced the influx of refugees.[24]

It took quite some time for concerns about immigration to produce any changes in policy, however. The default position of the United States from the beginning had been open borders. Not only did the founders place no restriction on immigration in the Constitution, but there was not a single serious restriction on immigration prior to the Chinese Exclusion Act of 1882.[25]

After the Civil War, moreover, anti-immigrant sentiment softened temporarily. Some of this stemmed from Lincoln's reinvigoration of liberalism. Northern liberals and Republicans took pride in the diversity of the nation, the idea that people from all walks of life came to the United States and produced an "American" out of the composite of different intermingled, international strains. "We are the Romans of the modern world," Oliver Wendell Holmes declared, "the great assimilating people."[26] Lincoln's Republican Party, which saw itself as rededicating the nation to the Declaration and the original principles of the Revolution, tended to welcome immigration. Northern industry benefited from cheap labor, and Northern politicians benefited from new voters. In ending slavery and freeing the slaves, Congress had also officially confirmed the original thoughts of Jefferson and other founders that anyone who arrived on American shores could be a citizen, and anyone who was born in America was automatically one—birthright citizenship, as it would be known. Nineteenth-century Democrats were in some ways even friendlier to immigrants. The Irish Catholic immigrants in the nineteenth century overwhelmingly joined the Democratic Party and became a critical constituency. (The two parties tended to wrestle for the more complex German vote— though many Germans were Catholic, most were Protestant, but they still wanted to be able to drink their beer.) When Woodrow Wilson later resisted restriction-ist measures, he had his huge Irish constituency in mind.

Some Americans embraced immigration. By the turn of the century, the idea of the United States as a "melt-ing pot" in which all races, religions, and ethnic groups intermingled to create a new idea of Americanism took hold in some quarters. Theodore Roosevelt, a longtime New York pol whose constituencies spanned the range from upper-crust Protestants like himself to Irish, Ger-mans, Jews, and every other New York ethnic voting bloc, loved to boast of his variegated heritage. "The En-glishman thinks of the German as an alien by race and innate disposition," he observed. But "I know better, for I have some English and some German blood in me, not to speak of other strains." If in Europe the Slav seemed destined to clash with the Teuton, Roosevelt argued with pride, "here in America the descendants of Slavonic immigrants become men precisely like ourselves."[27]

Roosevelt was one of the last spokesmen for the American "melting pot," however. By his time, even progressives were having second thoughts. Progressives, after all, were themselves overwhelmingly white and Protestant, and many shared the broader concern that immigration would dilute and degrade the Anglo-Saxon culture which so many believed was the essential foun-dation of American liberties. Progressivism thus became part of the larger national effort to control the influx and make the foreigners safe for America.[28]

Although the popular discontent began in response to the influx of Catholic immigrants, it eventually broadened to include almost all immigrants. Concern grew toward the end of the nineteenth century, as the latest waves of immigration came not primarily from Ireland, Germany, and Northern Europe but from Eastern and Southeastern Europe, and also from Asia. Asians were the one group that was excluded even by the post–Civil War legislation, which allowed the naturalization of all "white persons and persons of African descent," and thereby tacitly excluded those whose skin color was called "yellow." Hundreds of thousands of Asian immigrants already in the country were left in a no-man's-land as "aliens ineligible to citizenship." The Chinese Exclusion Act of 1882 reflected many things—concerns of white workers about competition for jobs and wages, and of white families in California worried about overcrowded classrooms—but at the core of this extreme exclusionist policy was simple racism.[29]

The "new" immigrants were even more troubling to white Protestant America. The myriad languages spoken, the endless varieties of poverty, the look and habits of the new immigrants, the differing religions—from Polish Catholics to Eastern Orthodox Slavs to Jews—and, above all, the massive numbers sent many white Protestants into a panic. In 1870, almost 90 percent of foreign-born Americans came from Northern and Western Europe; by 1920, as many as 45 percent of all foreign-born Americans were from Southern and Eastern Europe.

The fact that the millions of new immigrants settled chiefly in the cities also created problems. There was a growing cultural divide between a shrinking rural America and a growing urban population, a divide that remains just as pronounced today. The cities were always suspect to many Americans, even in the early republic, when the urban seaboard and the interior frontier clashed along any number of economic, political, and social fronts. The clogged cities of late-nineteenth- and early-twentieth-century America now teemed with migrants from the South, both Black and white, with Irish and Germans from the mid-nineteenth-century immigration, and now with the millions of refugees pouring in from Eastern and Southeastern Europe.

Pressure to shut the doors on immigration grew from the end of the nineteenth century and, along with it, pressure to establish more clearly who was and who was not an American. Celebrations of the American "melting pot" increasingly gave way to anxiety among white Protestants as to whether the American "character" and "culture" were being poisoned by the introduction of all these different cultural strains. Fear spread that the new, foreign population was riddled with radicals and anarchists.[30]

The result was a new kind of American "national-ism," which sought to ground American liberal democ-racy firmly in an Anglo-Saxon Protestant tradition—and not merely in the tradition but in the supposedly supe-rior racial characteristics of Anglo-Saxons. This was less an American nationalism than an Anglo-Saxon nation-alism. The burgeoning academic professions of anthro-pology, sociology, and psychology held that white people from Northern Europe, the tall, blond "Nordic" race, were superior to white people from Central Europe, the stocky "Alpine" race, and to the darker, more slender "Mediterranean" race, and never mind to Black people and Jews.[31] People were judged fit or not fit based on their ethnic and racial background.

The strength and reach of the eugenics movement has been conveniently forgotten in the American collec-tive memory of this period, but it was a powerful force in the American academy and in respectable elite intel-lectual circles. Every college biology textbook contained a chapter on eugenics. Over the course of the 1920s and '30s, thirty states passed compulsory sterilization laws, and some sixty thousand people regarded as disabled or mentally ill were sterilized by state authorities. Madison Grant, among America's most famous figures in the young field of anthropology, published his best-selling work, *The Passing of the Great Race,* in 1916, warning that the "new" immigrants were destroying the dominant "Nordic" stock that was responsible for all human progress. He recommended segregation of the inferior races in "ghettos" and argued that "a rigid system of selection through the elimination of those who are weak or unfit—in other words, social failures—would solve the whole question in one hundred years, as well as enable us to get rid of the undesirables who crowd our jails, hospitals, and insane asylums."[32] His book was reprinted many times in America and in multiple foreign languages, including German (Adolf Hitler called the book "my Bible"). As a leading advocate of eugenics, Grant was showered with medals from American institutions, and he served as a key adviser to the House Immigration Committee as it deliberated on how to restrict immigration.[33]

In 1920, another American eugenicist, Theodore Lothrop Stoddard, published a widely read book warning against racial intermixing, *The Rising Tide of Color Against White World-Supremacy.* A Harvard graduate and member in good standing of the American Historical Association and the American Political Science Association, Stoddard would remain widely respected, even after his role as an adviser to the Klan was revealed, until he reported from Germany in 1940 praising the Nazi eugenics program, which sterilized some 350,000 people, as helpfully "weeding out the worst strains in the Germanic stock in a scientific and truly humanitarian way."[34]

The tensions between racial eugenics and the liberal principles of the Revolution and the early republic were obvious. Some eugenicists disparaged the "fatuous belief in universal suffrage" and "the lust for equality." Science, after all, proved the inequality of the races, so how absurd to build a system around the myth of equality. *The Saturday Evening Post*, one of the most popular magazines in the 1920s, with a circulation between two and three million, ran articles warning that the continuing flow of Alpine, Mediterranean, and Semitic immigrants must inevitably produce "a hybrid race of people as worthless and futile as the good-for-nothing mongrels of Central America and Southeastern Europe."[35]

All this racial categorizing got an even bigger "scientific" boost when the IQ test was invented and given to millions of American men enlisted for the First World War. The results, published after the war, purported to show that men born in Northern Europe were the equal of native-born white people in intelligence, but those born in Latin and Slavic countries were inferior. As the

Princeton professor of psychology and later inventor of the SAT college admissions exam, Carl C. Brigham, concluded in his 1923 book, *A Study of American Intelligence*, "The intellectual superiority of our Nordic group over the Alpine, Mediterranean and negro groups has been demonstrated." This was, as John Higham put it, "the flowering time of the semi-scientific racism that had burgeoned in the decade before" World War One.[36]

Anti-Semitism had not been a notable feature of the early republic or even of mid-nineteenth-century America, but it grew virulent toward the end of the century as part of the overall effort to define America as an Anglo-Protestant nation. For one thing, the number of Jews climbed dramatically, from twenty thousand in 1830 to three hundred thousand in 1880, most of them from Germany and Central Europe, and then to as many as five million by 1930, the majority from Russia and Eastern Europe.[37] These "new" Jewish immigrants seemed far more alien than the relatively well-to-do German Jews who had arrived earlier. In response, well-off white Protestants sought to create a white aristocracy in the rich precincts. Average white Protestant Americans jumped on the anti-Semitic bandwagon as populists in both North and South, angry at "Wall Street" and bankers, whom they blamed for their distressed economic conditions, adopted the historical European Christian tendency to view Jews as money-grubbing Shylocks. After 1910, Jews faced increasing barriers to employment; job advertisements read "no Jews" and "white Protestants only," and Jews were all but barred from attending colleges, or medical and law schools, where strict quotas kept many of them out well into the 1930s.

This loss of confidence about the American powers of assimilation and absorption was part of a much larger loss of faith in liberalism itself. World War One marked a turning point. Whether it just happened to coincide with a rising tide of xenophobia, or whether it caused it, the war strengthened demands for protecting the "Nordic" strain in America from the poison of other racial strands.[38] By the 1920s, onetime liberal intellectuals like Reinhold Niebuhr and Walter Lippmann were explicitly abandoning liberalism as lacking the necessary "ruthlessness" to survive. "We need something less circumspect than liberalism to save the world," Niebuhr argued.[39] He turned temporarily to communism, Lippmann temporarily to conservatism.

Meanwhile, the average American, confronted with the kaleidoscope of alleged foreign threats—anarchists, communists, unpatriotic Germans and Irish, socialists, Jews, Italians—turned against all things foreign. Wilson and his League of Nations fell victim to this mood, actively and aggressively stirred up by Theodore Roosevelt in his last days, and by Henry Cabot Lodge and other Republicans. With shameless hypocrisy, these two leading internationalist Republicans now openly equated "internationalism" with Bolshevism and pointedly, and absurdly, singled out the Jewish Leon Trotsky as the evil genius behind it all. It was they, not the Taft Republicans of the 1930s, who began the anticommunist red-baiting and stoked the paranoia about "internationalists" and "globalists" at home and abroad seeking to undermine America—all for the purpose of defeating Wilson. Rather remarkably, even a century later, Republicans are still warning of "globalists" and "cosmopolitans."

Today the 1920s are remembered for the Jazz Age and three bland Republican presidents, including "Silent Cal" Coolidge. But though the presidents were silent, the 1920s were a high-water mark of antiliberalism, the highest until now. The 1920 election, in fact, brought an unprecedented nationwide conservative attack against liberalism and progressivism in all their forms. It was more like the 2016 election of Trump than any other American election. But instead of electing a charismatic demagogue like Trump, the Republican Party swept into complete control of all three branches of the federal government, led by Warren G. Harding, a genial, not especially ambitious man (for a politician) whom even his supporters regarded as a second-rater. That the election of 1920 produced this nobody of a president whom Americans barely remember today has hidden the fact that the election was a political and ideological tsunami.

The Ku Klux Klan of the 1920s became the ultimate symbol of the continuing vibrancy of the antiliberal tradition in America, spreading from the South to much of America. The new Klan's target was the whole collection of alien peoples and beliefs. Whereas the original Klan had stuck to its narrow mission in the South of keeping Black people down and liberal whites out, this second incarnation of the Klan broadened its geographical scope to include the whole country and broadened its targets to include Catholics and Jews. Viewing Jews as part of an international plot to control and weaken America—an argument popularized by Henry Ford with his 1920 publication, *The International Jew: The World's Foremost Problem*—Klan publications described the Jew "as a subversive radical, a Shylock seeking power through money, and a 'Christ-killing' monster of moral corruption." The Jews were also linked to the corruption and degradation of American cities. As one Oregon Klansman put it, "the Kikes" were "so thick" in some cities "that a white man can hardly find room to walk on the sidewalk."[40] One major difference between the original Klan and the second Klan was that the former permitted any white person to become a member but the second limited membership to white Protestants.[41] While racism against Black people remained the core of the Klan's appeal in the South, its successful spread to the Midwest and other regions of the country benefited from the inclusion of Catholics and Jews as the enemies of "real" America. As the Klan's Imperial Wizard, Hiram Wesley Evans, put it, "The Nordic American today is a stranger in . . . the land his fathers gave him . . . a most unwelcome stranger, one much spit upon, and one to whom even the right to have his own opinions and to work for his own interests is now denied with jeers and revilings."[42]

The second Klan originated in 1915, after the release of the D. W. Griffith movie starring Lillian Gish entitled *The Birth of a Nation*, which glorified the original Klan and its dashing leader, the former Confederate cavalry general Nathan Bedford Forrest. It was screened at the White House by an approving Woodrow Wilson. In less than a decade, the new Klan boasted a membership of five to six million, though the actual number was probably closer to three million. As important as the Klan's direct support was, its real success lay in its broad respectability in 1920s America. The original Klan operated in secrecy as a guerrilla organization continuing the Civil War by other means, using violence and terror under cover of night to kill opponents both Black and white. The Klan of the 1920s more resembled a racist national civic organization. It held its rallies in public and published recruiting ads in the newspapers; its members were proud and open about their affiliation, as were the politicians who worked to win their support. As Linda Gordon notes, "Far from appearing disreputable or extreme in its ideology, the 1920s Klan seemed ordinary and respectable to its contemporaries." Businessmen and professionals saw the Klan as a networking opportunity, not unlike the Rotary Club. Elected officials spoke at the Klan's events.[43] All kinds of people joined, including those, like Harry Truman and future Supreme Court Justice Hugo Black, who would later not only regret it but become champions of liberalism.

The great success of the Klan as a national organization revealed, among other things, the insecurity of middle-class white Protestants. It was not economic insecurity, however. The heyday of the second Klan, after all, came during the booming economy of the 1920s. The Klan had "no economic program" and revered "the pursuit of profit." Nor was the stereotype of Klan members as rural bumpkins accurate. Some 50 percent of members lived in cities, more than 30 percent in large cities. Klan members did blame "elites" for the nation's ills, but those elites were not the wealthy but the "big-city liberal professionals, secular urbanites who promoted cosmopolitanism" and who "looked down on Klanspeople as stupid and/or irrational and/or out of step with modernity." As Gordon observes, this disrespect for the Klan "only intensified its hostility and sense of righteousness."[44]

Mid-century liberal thinkers called it status anxiety, a response to "the entry into society of formerly 'disenfranchised' elements, particularly the children of immigrants and members of minority ethnic groups." It had been one thing when the newly arrived immigrants were at the bottom rung of society, despised and discriminated against, doing the "menial work" and playing "no important part in American politics," as Walter Lippmann observed in 1928. Their arrival had not yet challenged either the standing or the social and cultural worldview of the "dominant group" of "provincial" white Protestants. But then came the rise of the large cities, with their large populations of Catholics, Jews, and other immigrant groups. The booming economy of the 1920s allowed many of them to climb the economic ladder. Their presence in the increasingly influential cities gave them growing political clout as well, symbolized in 1924 by the Democratic presidential candidacy of the Catholic Al Smith from New York. As Seymour Martin Lipset observed, "The Klan, with its attack on metropolitan 'cosmopolitanism' and the more traditional minority ethnic scapegoats, seems to have provided an outlet to the frustrated residents of provincial America, who felt their values, power, and status slipping away."[45]

As Imperial Wizard Evans put it, "We are a movement of the plain people," who demanded "a return of power into the hands of the everyday, not highly cultured, not overly intellectualized, but entirely unspoiled and not de-Americanized, average citizen of the old stock."[46]

Like the antiliberal movements of the antebellum years, the Klan in the 1920s "functioned both inside and outside the electoral system." Outside the system, Klansmen employed violence against Black people, Catholics, and Jews, as well as enforcement among white Protestants of various moral codes. There was also significant political intimidation. "Many a candidate sought Klan support . . . out of fear of retribution."[47] At the same time, the Klan also exercised considerable muscle within the system. The 1924 Democratic National Convention could not approve a plank condemning the Klan, and the leading candidate at the time, William Gibbs McAdoo, refused to renounce the substantial Klan support he received against the other prospective nominee, the New York City Catholic Al Smith. In the mid-1920s, the Klan claimed seventy-five members of the House, including a majority of the Texas and Colorado delegations, sixteen senators, and eleven governors, about equally divided between Republicans and Democrats.[48]

The Klan wielded its considerable influence in Congress especially on the matter of immigration. The Immigration Act of 1924 was a culmination of restrictionist efforts going back at least two decades, but its passage reflected both the influence of the Klan and, more important, the broader mood of many Americans. Presidents and Congresses had repeatedly rejected efforts to tighten immigration by various means—Theodore Roosevelt had tried to contain anti-immigration sentiment in California; Wilson three times vetoed proposed literacy tests designed to keep out the uneducated rabble.[49] But the war and the disillusion that followed, the public weariness with progressive reforms, and a general desire of many Americans to enjoy what Harding called a "return to normalcy" now combined with growing anxiety about the floods of immigrants, which slowed appreciably during the war but quickly resumed as the war ended and millions of refugees sought escape from a devastated Europe.

The 1924 immigration legislation explicitly called for preserving the "racial preponderance" of "the basic strain of our population." The *Los Angeles Times* headline read "Nordic Victory Is Seen in Drastic Restrictions."[50] As one of the intellectual authors of the legislation put it, "The passage of the Immigration Act of 1924 marks the close of an epoch in the history of the United States." And so it did, the epoch begun by the founders, who had opened the doors to immigration both as a matter of principle and, they thought, for the betterment of the country.[51]

This would prove to be the high point of antiliberal-ism in the United States for some time. The effect would be to bring the percentage of foreign-born Americans to its lowest point in the twentieth century—just 8 per-cent in 1945, and just 4 percent by 1970, compared with a high of almost 15 percent in 1910. This was a dramatic accomplishment, but from the point of view of white Protestant restrictionists, it came far too late. The flow of immigrants who had already arrived in America were by the mid-1920s shifting the ideological and politi-cal balance of power dramatically in favor of the liberal tradition.

4

The Civil Rights Revolution

THE FIFTY MILLION immigrants who entered the United States after 1850 were a political and social reality that transformed the political, ideological, and social complexion of the country, and of the two major parties. Over the course of the 1920s and '30s, Republicans became more and more the party of white Protestant, nonurban America, while the Democratic Party became more and more a coalition of urban ethnic minorities plus, of course, the antiliberal racist South.[1] The starkest symbol of that transformation was the Democrats' nomination in 1928 of the urban New York Catholic Al Smith, who, although he lost in the general election to Herbert Hoover, revealed the ascendancy of the urban immigrant wing of the party. As one Democratic senator from South Carolina expressed the attitude of the Southern wing of the party to this novel development: "We have infected ourselves and our party with political miasma and pestilence, brought here from the fetid and sickening atmospheres of the old countries. . . . The Democratic Party must declare whether it will serve high, straight, outspoken American democracy or some kind of shambling, bastard, shame-faced mixture of so-called democracy and alien-conceived bolshevism or socialism or hell broth of all."[2] In the general election campaign, Southern Democrats abandoned their party in great numbers. Southern Protestant ministers warned that a vote for Smith was a vote "against Christ."[3]

There were many aspects of Al Smith's candidacy beyond his Catholicism that upset what Walter Lippmann called "the older American stocks," including what Smith represented: the new urban America with its corruptions and "clamorous" lifestyle, and, above all, its teeming immigrant population. But the progressive Republican senator from Nebraska, George Norris, saw clearly that Smith's Catholicism was what defeated him in the race with Hoover: "Regret it and conceal it as we may, religion had more to do with the defeat of Governor Smith than any other one thing."[4]

The results of the 1928 election nevertheless marked a significant shift. The immigrants, new and old, had lodged themselves firmly in the American political system and wielded influence commensurate with their voting power. Politicians courted their votes and were attentive to their concerns. The platforms of both parties paid at least lip service to immigrant interests.

At the same time, both parties were shifting their constituencies. Democrats increased their vote in the cities considerably, especially those with large concentrations of immigrants and Catholics.[5] Hoover, meanwhile, made unprecedented Republican inroads in the South. He carried Virginia and North Carolina, the first time a Republican had done so since 1872, and he carried Texas for the first time in history. These states would return to the Democratic column during the Roosevelt and Depression years, but the re-sorting of the two parties, which would eventually produce something like the present distributions of party power, had its roots in the 1920s. The Republican Party was becoming more and more the party of white Protestant America, while the Democratic Party was becoming the party of ethnic and racial minorities, with the antiliberal South an increasingly unhappy partner in an increasingly dysfunctional political marriage.

The economic crisis that struck America and the rest of the world in the 1930s also worked against the antiliberal forces that had been so dominant in the 1920s. The onset of the Great Depression badly discredited the conservative Republican dynasty that had dominated American politics since the end of the First World War. Not only did Franklin Roosevelt win the elections of 1932 and 1936 by massive margins—472–59 in the Electoral College in 1932, 523–8 in 1936—but the Senate, which had a 53–39 Republican majority in 1928, flipped to a 75–17 Democratic majority just eight years later. In the House, Republicans had enjoyed a 270–164 majority in 1928; by 1936, the Democrats had an overwhelming majority of 322–103. Republicans would retake both houses briefly in 1946, and win the presidency under Eisenhower, but not until the collapse of the Democratic Party over Vietnam in the 1970s and the subsequent rise of Ronald Reagan did antiliberal conservative Republicanism return to electoral viability. From the 1930s to the 1970s, antiliberal Republicans were a beleaguered minority.

The New Deal greatly expanded the role of the federal government in every aspect of national life. This spelled trouble for antiliberals. Although Roosevelt had few scruples about working with racist Southern Democrats, who would continue to be a valued part of his governing coalition, and did little to ease the plight of Black people in the South, the economic crisis turned everyone's attention temporarily away from racial, ethnic, religious, and cultural differences and toward class. Even the two great demagogues of the era, Huey Long and Father Charles Coughlin, began as enthusiastic supporters of Roosevelt and pushed redistributionist economic plans before the former was assassinated and the latter turned against Roosevelt and made anti-Semitism and isolationism his leading issues. The expansion of the federal government in the hands of an increasingly Northern-based Democratic Party could only work against antiliberal forces in the long run.

The discrediting of Republican antiliberal conservatism opened space for the groups struggling for equal rights and social position who had been at the mercy of white Protestant majorities in both parties. Now they found an opportunity in the opening of the Democratic Party, at least in the North. In the highly charged atmosphere of the Depression and war years, they also found an increasing number of white people committed to liberalism. Even in 1928, Al Smith's Democratic candidacy had strong support from prominent liberals of the day, including future Supreme Court Justice Felix Frankfurter, who was also the cofounder of the American Civil Liberties Union in 1920. As an editorial in *The Nation* put it, Smith's candidacy was itself a symbol to most intellectuals "of tolerance in American life—racial, religious, and social tolerance, accepting into the American family the city-dwellers who have come to us within the last century."[6]

For the first time in many years, a powerful working alliance was forged between oppressed Black people and immigrant groups and liberal white Protestants. The great engineer and symbol of that alliance was Franklin Roosevelt. The most patrician of white Protestant leaders, in his earlier career he had shown no particular interest in the rights of Black people or ethnic and religious minorities. Nevertheless, as leader of a Democratic Party increasingly catering to those constituencies, Roosevelt proved more than capable of creating the new, liberal-oriented Democratic Party.

Among the most obvious beneficiaries were American Jews. Not only did Jews vote overwhelmingly for Democrats in the cities, thereby ensuring that Democratic politicians would pay more attention to their concerns, but there were so many prominent Jews in Roosevelt's vaunted "brain trust" that some critics took to calling it the "Jew Deal."

Yet Catholics also benefited. The Depression helped energize the most liberal elements of twentieth-century Catholicism—namely, those devoted to assisting the poor and disadvantaged against an uncaring and, at best, amoral capitalist system. Here was one place where the Catholic critique of liberal individualism temporarily meshed with popular views. The collective, government-centered response of the New Deal was more in keeping with Catholic teachings than the "rugged individualism" of unfettered capitalism. In 1931, Pope Pius XI released his encyclical *Quadragesimo Anno*, in which he declared that "the right ordering of economic life cannot be left to a free competition of forces."[7] Two years later, Dorothy Day, a radical anarchist convert to Catholicism, began the Catholic Worker Movement, which aimed, among other things, to relieve the plight of the downtrodden.

The prominent Catholic theologian and social activist John A. Ryan had long criticized liberal capitalist individualism and promoted collective solutions to economic and social problems. He became such a prominent supporter of Roosevelt's New Deal policies that he was sometimes called "Monsignor New Deal."

Remarkably, even Black people began to shake their longtime attachment to the party of Lincoln. Much of this was due to a deliberate strategy of Republicans. By the 1920s, the party was split at the state level between the "black-and-tan" faction, which wanted to continue courting Black votes as part of the traditional Republican coalition going back to the Civil War, and the "lily-whites," who wanted to purge the party of Black leaders to appeal to white voters, especially in the South. By the time of Hoover's 1928 campaign, the lily-whites were winning in the states; Black people were removed from prominent positions in the party. Even though Roosevelt's Democratic Party remained heavily influenced by its racist Southern wing, Roosevelt himself began courting Black votes more determinedly and effectively than any previous Democrat. The change was quickly apparent. The Black vote, which remained overwhelmingly Republican even in 1932, shifted to the Democrats in 1936, a further blow to Southern white domination of the party.

World War Two dealt the most devastating blow of

all to all the different strains of antiliberalism—racial, ethnic, and religious. The effect of the war on the ongoing struggle between liberalism and antiliberalism was visible on several fronts. First was the nature of the enemy. That Hitler was the ultimate promoter of the racist views that had grown so popular in the United States was not lost on contemporaries. The Nazi implementation of eugenics policies, the institutionalization and militarization of "Nordic" supremacy, so badly discredited the vast and influential school of eugenics in the United States that Americans today barely know such a thing existed. The respected academics who held such views either abandoned them, repudiated them, or lost respectability. Many conservative Republicans in the 1930s had been sympathetic to, or at least not unduly troubled by, the Nazis' policies, including their persecution of Jews. That view was also discredited. After 1941, such news about the Holocaust as reached America discredited anti-Semitism and forced those who held anti-Semitic views—probably a majority of the American population—to keep them largely to themselves. In short, the whole intellectual edifice of antiliberal white supremacy, which had dominated the American academy, American intellectual circles, and the general prejudices of average white Protestants, was badly damaged by the war with German racism.

Catholics also benefited from the war in their struggle for equal rights and against discrimination. In making the case for American involvement, Roosevelt had emphasized, above all else, religious freedom. In the late 1930s, that was often a euphemism for opposing Nazi persecution of Jews, but other religious minorities benefited from the reassertion of the principle—as a war aim, no less. Indeed, the first two of Roosevelt's "Four Freedoms" in January 1941 were a restatement of the First Amendment—"freedom of speech and expression" and "the freedom of every person to worship in his own way." What Roosevelt added, with a perhaps unconscious nod to Lincoln, was that people should be able to enjoy these freedoms "everywhere in the world"—i.e., regardless of nationality, religion, or race.

The experience of the war undermined the idea of racial hierarchies in a more basic way. The clichéd World War Two image of the Irish, Jewish, Italian, and Southern boys all fighting together and getting past their old prejudices undoubtedly exaggerated reality. But the "melting pot" metaphor, abandoned by the 1920s, returned to favor. There would be no more discussion in polite company of the inherent superiority of the "Nordic" to the "Alpine" and "Mediterranean" races. There would be much necessary adjustment in the language and mores of respectable society—a "wokeness" *avant la lettre*—as people were gradually forced to stop calling Jewish Americans "Kikes," Italian Americans "Wops," and Irish Americans "Micks" and otherwise wearing their religious and ethnic prejudices on their sleeves.

The church in Rome had famously been sympathetic to the fascist governments in the 1930s, partly because of the treatment of Catholics by Spanish Republicans and communists in the Spanish Civil War. And prominent Catholics in the United States, led by Father Coughlin, were outraged at Americans' lack of concern for their persecuted Catholic brethren overseas. But those memories of Catholic support for fascism abroad were significantly washed out by Catholic Americans' participation in the war. If white Protestants could form a "band of brothers" with their Irish American or Italian American fellow soldiers, then the latter's Catholic religion was obviously no obstacle. This hardly did away with anti-Catholicism in America, as would become clear when the next Catholic candidate ran for president in 1960, but it submerged it as a passionate cause for most Protestant Americans.

Wartime employment threw everyone together, including, of course, bringing millions of women into the workforce, inevitably redefining the roles of the sexes. The wartime manufacturing boom accelerated the migration of Black people from Southern farms to Northern factories and cities. The number of Black people employed in manufacturing increased from five hundred thousand to 1.2 million during the war, in addition to the 1.2 million Black men and women who served in various positions in the armed forces. Though they were blocked from serving in combat roles at first, and lived in segregated facilities throughout the war, they gradually had a chance to prove themselves in combat as the need for more manpower at the front lines grew toward the end of the war. The more Black people contributed to the war effort, the more many felt emboldened to demand an end to the government's official discrimination against them. As one leader of the NAACP put it in 1942, "no Negro leader" could ask fellow Black people to support the war so long as they were discriminated against by the very same government that called for their service. As for those who did serve overseas, they expected to return to a better America. In 1945, one Alabama corporal stated, "I spent four years in the Army to free a bunch of Dutchmen and Frenchmen, and I'm hanged if I'm going to let the Alabama version of the Germans kick me around when I get home."[8]

All these factors combined to produce a dramatic shift in the balance of power back toward the liberal tradition established by the founders. The number of groups energized to seek or at least acquiesce in extending and protecting the rights of oppressed minorities was larger than at any time since the Civil War, and before that the Revolution. No small part of the liberal gains in this period was due simply to the crumbling of the old

immovable wall of religious, ethnic, and racial antiliberalism. It was not that the South ceased to resist and to
fight for its antiliberal position, but it was increasingly
isolated, and the dominance it had still enjoyed in the
1920s was gone. With that powerful obstacle removed,
new groups seeking equality in the American system had
more room to maneuver and to make use of the tools
provided by the founders for pressing for their rights.
Part of this revolution was circumstantial—the Depression, the war, and their effect on electoral politics—but
the rest was a matter of appealing to the liberal ideals
of the founding and making use of the principles of the
Declaration, the Bill of Rights, and the "purified" post–
Civil War Constitution.

This shift was obvious enough that a Swedish soci-
ologist, Gunnar Myrdal, wrote a widely respected book
in 1944 called *The American Dilemma*. The dilemma,
of course, concerned the gap between the "American
Creed" of equal rights and the continuing reality of
American racial oppression. Whatever many American
white people might prefer, the Black people of America
were no longer going to be "patient" and "submissive."
Having gained a measure of freedom and, in the North,
the ability to influence politics, they were not going to
cease pressing. They would increasingly become less easily "accommodated." They would "organize for defense
and offense" and become "more and more vociferous."[9]

In fact, Black leaders had been organizing for decades to push back against their almost complete disenfranchisement by Southern states, and against the broader, pervasive oppression of the Jim Crow laws. The NAACP, founded in 1909, tried futilely over its first three decades to challenge institutionalized racism by legal means, bringing court cases against the South's "white primaries," which had been established throughout the South after 1900 and excluded Black people from voting in the all-important Democratic Party primaries.[10] The scholar W. E. B. Du Bois called for "ceaseless agitation" using all peaceful methods of protest, lobbying, and litigation.[11]

It was only in the 1940s, in the much-changed political climate of the war years, that some of these efforts began to show success. In 1941, Philip Randolph threatened a "march on Washington" if the government did not do something about anti-Black discrimination in the military and in government employment more generally. Roosevelt appointed more than a hundred Black people to administrative posts, and the number of Black federal employees tripled in the 1930s. The Roosevelt administration also desegregated most federal facilities, including restrooms and cafeterias. In 1941, Roosevelt signed an executive order prohibiting racial discrimination in the defense industry and establishing the Fair Employment Practices Commission to ensure equal opportunity for Black people. In 1944, the Supreme Court ruled the South's "white primaries" unconstitutional; in 1946, it declared segregation on interstate buses unconstitutional; and in 1948, it outlawed racially segregated housing practices. In 1948, Harry Truman issued an executive order ending racial segregation in the armed forces. Two years later, Thurgood Marshall and the NAACP's Legal Defense Fund scored major victories in three cases in which the Supreme Court began to chip away at the "separate but equal" doctrine of *Plessy v. Ferguson*. By 1954, after careful work by the chief justice, Earl Warren, to achieve a unanimous decision, the court finally overturned the 1896 ruling and declared that separate was inherently unequal. This decision, in *Brown v. Board of Education*, was a decisive turning point in terms of the law, although whether the court's ruling would be implemented and enforced remained to be seen.

These developments revealed the dramatic shift in the balance of power between the liberal and antiliberal traditions. Every step toward recognizing the equal rights of Black people in the law was slow, painful, controversial, and bitterly contested, and met with opposition, both legal and illegal, including mass violence, chiefly though not exclusively against Black people. But the movement toward greater and greater fulfillment of the liberal principles of the Revolution and early republic was relentless, certainly from the Southern point of view. The Southern Democratic Party and the conservative antiliberal white Protestant forces in the Republican Party had been the twin pillars of the antiliberal movement. But between the Depression and the war, the conservative antiliberal wing of the Republicans had been widely discredited and pushed to the fringe. The dominant forces in the party were now moderate and liberal. The first Republican president since 1928, Dwight D. Eisenhower, had considered running as a Democrat. His instincts were those of a Northern conservative. He did not especially care about Black rights and would not even support the *Brown* decision publicly; he showed great concern for Southern feelings and worried that pushing things too far too fast would tear the country apart: "It's all very well to talk about school integration," he once commented, but "you may also be talking about social disintegration."[12]

Whatever Eisenhower's personal and political desire to balance the demands of the South against the demands of liberals in both parties, however, he was operating in circumstances in which liberalism for the moment had the upper hand. The alliance of Black people and sympathetic liberal white people in both parties had more clout than the alliance of Southern and Northern antiliberals in both parties. Eisenhower's appointment of Earl Warren as chief justice confirmed the new balance of power. Warren was a Republican from the sizable liberal end of the party. Although Eisenhower had not anticipated Warren's role in *Brown*, and would regret it, choosing Warren was a way of cementing the support of the party's liberal wing. Even Richard Nixon, the closest thing there was to a conservative in the top ranks of the party, would turn in 1960 to a liberal Republican stalwart, and New Yorker, Nelson Rockefeller, for endorsement in what became known as the "Compact of Fifth Avenue," a symbolic death knell to the anti-urban, anti-Northeastern, anti-secular, anti-elite Republican conservatives who had dominated the party before 1940.

The Democratic Party, meanwhile, continued its shift away from Southern domination—or, rather, the South became increasingly uncomfortable in a Democratic Party that was catering to immigrants and non-white people. The 1948 Democratic Convention saw the party split wide open. On one side, the Southern antiliberals fought against civil rights planks, insisted the federal government was moving too quickly and with insufficient concern for Southern rights and interests, and threatened to bolt from the party. Soon after the convention, some Southern Democrats did indeed rebel and formed the Dixiecrat or States' Rights Party, under the leadership of the South Carolina Democrat and future Republican, Strom Thurmond. The Dixiecrats went on to win more than a million popular and thirty-nine electoral votes, which almost handed the Republicans a victory over Truman in 1948. But, overall, Southern influence in the party was weakening. Northern liberals were in the ascendant, as they had never been since the party's founding over a century before. At the 1948 convention, the mayor of Minneapolis, Hubert Humphrey, declared, "To those who say we are rushing this issue of civil rights, I say to them we are 172 years too late. To those who say that this civil rights program is an infringement on states' rights, I say this: The time has arrived in America for the Democratic Party to get out of the shadows of states' rights and walk forthrightly into the bright sunshine of human rights."[13]

By the time the court handed down its antisegregation ruling in 1954, a strong liberal consensus had developed across both parties. A new, more liberal Democratic Party controlled the White House, and the Republican Party's moderate liberal wing dominated its conservative wing. Liberals controlled all three branches of the federal government at a time when the power and authority of the federal government was at its highest because of the New Deal, World War Two, and then the Cold War. Put another way, the North was in charge in a way it had not been since the election of Lincoln.[14]

The Southern antiliberals would not go down without a fight. The *Brown* decision and the subsequent pressures from both Black and white people sparked a rebellion in the South much like the Nullification Crisis of 1832, the secession of 1860, and, later, the effectual nullification of the Civil War amendments following the end of Reconstruction. To many Americans outside the South, it was extraordinary how little the South had changed over the course of a century in which so much else had changed. The common view in the North, articulated both by Eisenhower and by the Democratic presidential nominee, Adlai Stevenson, was that the people of the South needed time to adjust, as if just living in the American liberal democratic system would over time acculturate them to accept liberalism.

Here again was a central conceit of liberalism, inherited from the Enlightenment, the idea that with time and education, with science and reason, all people must eventually make their way up the ladder of civilization to liberalism. Mid-century liberal thinkers saw antiliberal conservatism less as an ideological alternative to liberalism than as a bad adjustment to what they called "modernity," with "modernity" itself defined in part by the triumph of liberalism. The "backlash" theory, which was essentially how Eisenhower saw the problem, held that the white people of the South had to be brought along slowly and carefully, with the underlying assumption that they would eventually get there on their own if not provoked by a hurried "radicalism."

But this notion of inevitable moral progress upward toward liberalism was and is a figment of the liberal imagination, as the South has proved again and again over the course of two and a half centuries. In fact, in 1954 the great majority of white Southerners hadn't changed their views at all since the Civil War. Preserving white supremacy was as important to white Southerners then as it had been in 1865. Public opinion polls showed that 80 percent of white Southerners opposed school desegregation. Southern political leaders frankly warned that the South would not obey the decisions of the court.

Immediately following the *Brown* decision, Southern states enacted hundreds of laws to prevent or limit desegregation, forcing schools and public pools to close rather than fulfill court orders, revoking the licenses of teachers who taught mixed classes, and in some cases effectively abolishing public schools in favor of state-supported private schools. As Harvard Sitkoff notes, "Defiance of the court and the constitution became the touchstone of southern loyalty, the necessary proof of one's concern for the security of the white race."[15] In 1956, 101 Southern members of Congress signed a "Declaration of Constitutional Principles" that became known as the "Southern Manifesto" and called on states to refuse to obey the desegregation order on the grounds that only the states, not the court or the federal government, could decide such matters. This was exactly the position Southern leaders took at the time of the founding; it was the South's position in the antebellum years; it was the

South's position during and after Reconstruction; and it remained the South's position in the "modern" America of the 1950s and '60s.

Once again, the antiliberal forces fought outside as well as inside the political and legal system. The Klan reemerged and was joined by White Citizens' Councils and other vigilante groups that intimidated and, in some cases, murdered Black people seeking to register to vote, including the sensational killing at his home of the Mississippi civil rights activist Medgar Evers. Mobs of white protesters screamed, cursed, spat on, and threw rocks at Black children trying to enter schools. White students were encouraged to harass their Black classmates. Schools were dynamited. White civil rights activists from the North were also murdered, and the trials for these crimes invariably resulted in innocent verdicts by white Southern juries effectively engaging in nullification.

Yet the Southern white supremacy movement by this point was outgunned and outflanked. A new and powerful force had entered the picture. The willingness of Black people to risk life and limb drove the new revolution. Black Southerners began pressing on the white supremacist societal and legal "rules" that had governed their lives. They challenged rules about where Black people could sit on buses; young Black men and women challenged whites-only rules in public restaurants; Black leaders pressed for voting rights. In every situation, they risked severe injury and death at the hands of white mobs and vigilante groups. As Martin Luther King Jr. put it, a Black person had to be "willing to risk martyrdom in order to move and stir the conscience of his community and the nation." Rather than submit to "surreptitious cruelty in thousands of dark jail cells and on countless shadowed street corners," the Black citizen must "force his oppressor to commit his brutality openly . . . with the rest of the world looking on."[16]

The willingness of Black people to sacrifice their lives had an even more powerful effect on white Northerners than the abolitionist martyrs of the nineteenth century. The beatings and killings of peaceful Black men, women, and children protesters, the sight of innocent people being set upon by men on horseback with rubber truncheons wrapped in barbed wire, the dogs surging at women and children—these sacrifices of Black lives, and the brutality of their white oppressors, shown across the nation on people's television sets, had a profound effect on Northern opinion. As Sitkoff observes, "Time and again . . . such racist extremism would discredit the cause of the white South and force a majority of otherwise unconcerned citizens to demand that their federal government act," if only to preserve law and order.[17]

That the final blow to Southern political power

was dealt by a Southern Democratic president, Lyndon Johnson, showed how far the fortunes of antiliberalism had fallen. Johnson had not begun his career in Texas politics as a staunch defender of Black rights, but as a savvy politician he soon realized that, to win in a party that had nominated the Illinois governor Adlai Stevenson twice in the 1950s and then elected a liberal Catholic from Massachusetts as president in 1960, he was going to have to come out in favor of civil rights. Like Eisenhower before him, he tried to compromise and avoid direct confrontations with his fellow Southerners, but was ultimately driven squarely to oppose the South's dominant antiliberalism.

He did so in a way that was especially painful to the great majority of white Southerners. In signing into law the Voting Rights Act of 1965, which gave the federal Justice Department oversight of Southern state elections to ensure their openness and fairness to Black people, he gave a paean not to white generosity but to Black courage and Black virtue. Comparing the recent defiance of Black people against the racists of Selma, Alabama, to the battles at Lexington and Concord, Johnson told a joint session of Congress that the "real hero of this struggle" was the "American Negro. His actions and protests, his courage to risk safety, and even to risk his life, have awakened the conscience of this nation. His demonstrations have been designed to call attention to injustice, designed to provoke change, designed to stir reform. He has called upon us to make good the promise of America. And who among us can say that we would have made the same progress were it not for his persistent bravery and his faith in American democracy?" Johnson concluded, "This cause must be our cause too. It is not just Negroes, but all of us, who must overcome the crippling legacy of bigotry and injustice. And we *shall* overcome."[18]

5

The Birth of the "New" Right

THE PROGRESS OF civil rights in the 1950s and '60s and the broad liberal consensus in both parties seemed so strong that many concluded that antiliberal conservatism in America was dead, if it had ever existed at all. Mid-century liberal commentators like Daniel Bell and Richard Hofstadter treated the conservatives of their era as fringe holdovers from an earlier time, like Japanese soldiers still fighting the Second World War in island caves. This "Radical Right," as they called it, needed to be explained psychologically more than ideologically, as the product of "authoritarian personalities." They even referred to this right as "pseudo-conservative," borrowing from Theodor Adorno—not truly conservative in the sense of wanting to preserve institutions and traditions, but revolutionary in its hostility to the existing system. Louis Hartz crystallized this thinking in his widely read 1955 book, *The Liberal Tradition in America*.

Hartz argued that there was no genuine conservative dissenting tradition in America, by which he meant no European-style conservatism, because there had never been feudalism and the kind of traditional class structure that had produced revolution in France. American conservatives could not seek a return to the *ancien régime,* as European antiliberal critics like Joseph de Maistre did in the early nineteenth century, because in America there was no *ancien régime* to return to. In the United States, the Revolution and the early republic *were* the *ancien régime.* The only conservatism in America, in other words, was a "liberal" conservatism—a distinctly American conservatism dedicated to preservation of a distinctly American liberalism.

In fact, however, antiliberalism was still alive as an ideological force, even if it had fallen into minority status in both parties because of the dramatic events of the 1930s and '40s. Beginning in the 1950s, a new conservative intellectual movement took shape that did not wish to play the role Hartz assigned to it, as the guardian of the liberal inheritance. The leading thinkers of this school, the young William F. Buckley and the more established conservative thinker Russell Kirk, were both antiliberal on the issues of the day, and although Buckley claimed to be fighting against what he and others regarded as the distortions and excesses of modern

American liberalism—to stand "athwart history, yelling Stop!"—it was not alleged liberal excesses but the core of American liberalism that he and his colleagues opposed.

The supposedly "new" conservative movement that Buckley did more than anyone to construct in the 1950s and '60s picked up where the conservative antiliberalism of the 1920s had left off, defending white supremacy. Buckley's *National Review* throughout its first decade was a bastion of support for the South's resistance to desegregation. Its August 1957 editorial, "Why the South Must Prevail," argued that the "white community" of the South was "entitled" to continue discriminating against Black people because it was, "for the time being . . . the advanced race."[1]

What made Buckley such an influential figure in the conservative movement was the way he framed the issues. He portrayed efforts to bring the South in line with the principles of the Declaration as "radical social experimentation." He dressed up conservative antiliberalism as a Burkean respect for history and tradition. He attacked liberals for imposing "ideological abstractions about equality" against the South's traditions. The *Brown* decision was a case of a liberal court run amok, he argued, "imposing *its* will on the folkways and mores of the nation." The difference between a conservative and a liberal, Buckley argued, was that the conservative "feels a sympathy for the Southern position which the Liberal, applying his ideological abstractions ruthlessly, cannot feel."[2]

This was the classic European antiliberal critique of liberalism, ostensibly justified by a Burkean respect for tradition. It was not the American Revolutionary tradition to which Buckley and his allies appealed, however, but a tradition of Anglo-Protestant white supremacy that predated the Revolution. The Warren Court, after all, was not pulling liberal abstractions out of the air; they were the liberal abstractions of the Declaration of Independence. The court was not attacking a long-settled status quo with innovative interpretations of the Constitution. It was not creating "new rights." It was simply removing some more of the many "shackles," as Jefferson described them, that had not been removed by the Constitution and the Civil War. When Buckley claimed to be standing "athwart history, yelling Stop!," therefore, it was not history as of 1957; it was history as of 1776.

Part of Buckley's aim was to wrap the fight against desegregation into a broader fight against the New Deal and the growth of government. The problem with the *Brown* decision, Buckley complained, was that this imposition of "an abstract concept" would send America "down a road towards omnipotent government." This was nothing more than a repackaging of the old South's insistence that the federal government had no business meddling in its affairs, but Buckley gave it a new and seemingly loftier rationale.[3]

Railing against "omnipotent government" was generally a winner in American politics and could attract many conservative followers who did not necessarily share Buckley's and the "new" conservatives' racism. In the early Cold War era, the alleged war on "big government" allowed conservatives to tie a number of disparate issues into a political program that could hold a coalition of conservatives, both liberal and antiliberal, together. Opposition to "omnipotent government," anticommunism, and the defense of "traditional" values, by which were meant chiefly white, Christian values—these became the three pillars of conservatism from Buckley to Ronald Reagan. Indeed, much of conservative politics throughout the Cold War decades, and even today, lay in deliberately blurring the distinction between liberalism and communism, suggesting that the imposition of liberal principles, including those established by the Declaration and Bill of Rights, was akin to the totalitarian impositions of the communists and even of the Nazis. Not just Southern white supremacists but the Irish Catholic Joseph McCarthy and the Protestant John Birch Society all accused Eisenhower of being a communist, or at least of pursuing pro-communist policies. Meanwhile, Black civil rights activists like Martin Luther King Jr. were also treated as communists whether or not they were involved with the inconsequential American Communist Party.

As potent as these ideas eventually became in reviving antiliberal conservatism in the 1980s and beyond, as a political force antiliberal conservatism remained weak from the 1950s through the 1970s. The overwhelming support Eisenhower received in the 1952 and 1956 elections showed that the majority of Republican voters did not strongly oppose either the New Deal or, outside the South, desegregation. Buckley and other conservatives rightly regarded Eisenhower as an enemy, but the problem for them was that Eisenhower was the most consistently popular Republican since Theodore Roosevelt. The closest thing to a respectable political spokesman for Buckley's conservatism was Robert Taft, a quadrennial loser in presidential contests since 1940, unable even to win his own party's nomination. Less respectable, but more politically successful, was Joe McCarthy, whom Buckley championed long after he was disowned not only by Eisenhower but even by the onetime McCarthyite Richard Nixon.

It has been a common complaint among antiliberal conservatives over the past decade that the two parties are part of the same liberal establishment—the "uniparty," as Senator Josh Hawley likes to put it. That was how antiliberal conservatives felt throughout the 1950s, 1960s, and well into the 1970s. The *National Review's* readers consistently opposed Eisenhower. Even though Nixon often played to the white South and to white ethnics across the country—his "silent majority"—antiliberal conservatives wrote off Nixon, or, perhaps more accurately, he wrote them off, when he made his pact with the liberal Republican Rockefeller in 1960. "A choice, not an echo," was the conservative hero Barry Goldwater's campaign slogan in 1964, an explicit criticism of Eisenhower/Nixon Republicanism, but his landslide defeat seemed to be the final signal to antiliberal conservatives that even Republican voters did not insist on a stark antiliberal conservative alternative. It was Nixon again after 1968; throughout his presidency, he courted liberals, seeking détente with the Soviet communists and opening relations with "Red" China, and, far from unwinding the New Deal and Lyndon Johnson's Great Society programs, adding new government programs of his own. Conservatives stuck by Nixon on the Vietnam War and took his side against the growing left and the antiwar movement, but they had long since stopped regarding him as one of them.

Throughout these decades, therefore, the antiliberal conservatives lacked a powerful national leader, or even a sympathetic leadership in either party. The millions of Southerners, bitter about the federal government's repeated, direct intervention on behalf of Black people, under both Republican and Democratic presidents, increasingly looked for an alternative source of leadership and protection against the liberal onslaught. They were joined by both Northern and Southern religious Protestants more and more unhappy as the Warren Court began to enforce more stringently the founders' clear instructions separating church and state. The turning point for religious conservatives came in 1962, when the Supreme Court ruled that school-sponsored prayer in public schools violated the establishment clause of the First Amendment. In the 1950s and '60s, this antiliberal coalition made up the bulk of McCarthy's supporters and filled the ranks of the John Birch Society. In the 1964 election, many of these antiliberal conservatives, in North and South, flocked to George Wallace. The antiliberal forces in the country could still be counted in the millions, but they lacked a foothold in the main political competition.

The complaints of these groups were not primarily economic—the 1950s and '60s, like the 1920s, were boom times in the American economy, and membership in antiliberal groups like the John Birch Society spanned all economic levels. Liberal sociologists and political thinkers of the day still attributed their dissent from American liberalism to status anxiety. In particular, the new skills required for success in the late stages of the "second industrial revolution" depended increasingly on higher education, leaving those with older skill sets and a secondary-school education suddenly ill-equipped to compete, and not just with better-educated white people but also with the children of immigrants advancing through the American education system. This "reworking the social map of the country, upsetting the established life chances and outlooks of old privileged groups, and creating uncertainties about the future," the liberal sociologists believed, was what fueled the passions of the "radical right."[4] The world was changing too fast for these simple people to comprehend and adjust to; with time and education, they would. "Modernity," after all, was a reality that could not be evaded.

There was some truth to this rather condescending view—and the political and ideological gap between the college-educated and non-college-educated would grow ever wider over the coming decades. But this analysis elided or ignored a more basic truth, which was that these people were not just responding to circumstances. They were fundamentally antiliberal in their outlook. Rich or poor, successful or unsuccessful, well educated or not, they simply did not believe in human equality or universal natural rights when it came to certain groups— Black people, in particular—and they took active steps to resist the imposition of those liberal beliefs on them. It was not modernity that they objected to; it was the advancing hegemony of the American liberal tradition bequeathed by the Revolution and the founders.

That hegemony had expanded significantly by the time Buckley wrote and would continue to expand over the coming decades. Claims of racial superiority had been discredited by the Nazis and could no longer be expressed in the old language of white supremacy. The immigration of the 1890s to the 1920s had created vast new constituencies for liberal reform. And three decades of liberal government and New Deal policies had created what C. Wright Mills in his 1956 book, *The Power Elite,* called the "new class": lawyers, journalists, university professors, the experts who flocked to government beginning in the 1930s. This new class was predominantly liberal, since such professions depended on liberalism to survive. The rise of the new class to positions of power in the economy and political system strengthened an increasingly liberal trend in government, politics, and society. As Daniel Bell put it in 1962, the New Deal had "rewoven" the very "fabric of government . . . with liberal thread."[5]

This liberal hegemony was so firmly ensconced after the 1950s that when the "Reagan Revolution" arrived in 1980, it did not revolutionize things as much as many antiliberal conservatives hoped and many liberals feared. Reagan's victory did return antiliberal conservatives to positions of power for the first time since the 1920s, and, perhaps more important, gave them the feeling that they were finally being listened to, which encouraged them to organize and expand their efforts to push back against the liberal onslaught. Many of the institutions that would later play a role in the takeover of the Republican Party in 2016 were hatched and nurtured during the Reagan years.

Reagan's election owed less to the triumph of antiliberal conservatism, however, than to a collapse within liberalism. The Vietnam War fractured the liberal establishment of both parties, and there was general public disenchantment with the Great Society programs and the "welfare state" as it had evolved by the late 1970s. This disenchantment had a potent racial component, which Reagan and other Republican politicians exploited— brandishing the racially loaded stereotype of the "welfare queen." But it was not just racists who believed that the anti-poverty programs of the 1960s and '70s weren't accomplishing their declared purpose. Bill Clinton, whom many Black people at the time regarded as the "first Black president," did the most to "reform" welfare, and in his 1996 second inaugural address declared, "The era of big government is over."

Disgruntlement with the welfare state was not a victory for antiliberalism, although Buckley and other conservatives used their attack on the New Deal and later social programs in their assault on liberalism. In fact, the founders had not specified how much government involvement in the economy was too much or too little.

On the one hand, they did believe deeply in the importance of property, because, following Locke, they believed that if people owned nothing, if government or society or the community controlled everything, from a person's land to the clothes on a person's back, then what could a person call his own? What aspect of a person's life and being was off limits to the state? The "rights of persons" and the "rights of property," Madison argued, "cannot be separated." Government was "instituted to protect property of every sort; as well that which lies in the various rights of individuals."[6] It would have been extraordinary if the founders had not believed in the importance of property in this sense. The idea of communal ownership was not prevalent at the time of the Revolution, nor had it ever found many adherents throughout recorded history prior to the Bolshevik Revolution (the Anabaptists of sixteenth-century Mün-ster come to mind.) Even the French revolutionaries believed in private property. So did the founders. Those Americans, generally on the left, who have viewed the founders' Lockean convictions as a problem that needs to be remedied may be right or wrong from some other philosophical and moral perspective, but such a view was fundamentally at odds with the liberal principles and the liberal system that the founders erected to protect them.

On the other hand, the founders were not property fetishists. None of them believed the government should have no role in the economy. They believed in tariffs and taxes, and not only to raise revenue but to protect American producers from foreign competition. Hamilton's economic program was a deliberate bit of social engineering, designed to gain the allegiance of the owners of capital to the new government. Jefferson's vision aimed at strengthening the "yeoman" farmer. But both aimed at liberal goals. Many in the revolutionary period did worry about the consequences of too much wealth, luxury, and inequality on "republican virtue." They understood that excessive wealth in the hands of the few could give that few a power threatening to a democratic republic, that vast inequalities in means were a problem for a society dedicated to the proposition of universal equality. But the founders took no steps to limit wealth other than to permit taxes. They knew there would be fights about taxes and other financial issues that would pit the few against the many. Their system was designed to allow that conflict to occur while as much as possible safeguarding the rights of all concerned.

Reagan's victory, in short, was not a defeat for liberalism. And the conservative antiliberals knew it. While Reagan waged a faux war on government and duked it out with liberal Democrats over foreign policy, the Republican Party's antiliberal faction had to be satisfied with crumbs from the table. It was true that antiliberals had more purchase in the Reagan administration than they had had in the Nixon and Eisenhower administrations. On the matter of Supreme Court jurisprudence, for instance, Reagan did begin the shift to the more conservative and antiliberal court that exists today. His appointment of Antonin Scalia, in particular, gave a boost to the jurisprudence of "originalism," which, although hardly new, aimed at reversing the Warren Court's liberal decisions. But he also appointed Sandra Day O'Connor and Anthony Kennedy, both of whom wrote or concurred in decisions recognizing women's rights, abortion rights, and gay rights. He chose George H. W. Bush, a liberal conservative, for his running mate—the 1980 equivalent of the "Compact of Fifth Avenue"—and he made James Baker, a famously "pragmatic" liberal conservative, his first chief of staff, and George P. Shultz, a Nixon man whom antiliberal conservatives disliked and mistrusted, his secretary of state. Reagan's cooperative relationship with the Democratic Speaker of the House, Tip O'Neill, was legendary. Reagan tried to portray himself as the president of all Americans regardless of party or ideology, and his reputation today, even among Democrats, suggests that he was not entirely unsuccessful.[7] As the historian Gary Gerstle observes, Reagan "lived comfortably within a Republican Party that was overwhelmingly white and native born and seems not to have been unsettled by his party's periodic attempts to demonize blacks."[8] Though Reagan was comfortable with the anti-liberal conservatives in his coalition, he was not one of them. His handpicked successor, George H. W. Bush, "had few close ties to the conservative movement." In 1992, the *National Review* endorsed Patrick Buchanan over Bush in the Republican primaries. Buchanan himself quit the Republican Party in disgust a few years later.[9]

By the time Reagan left office, in fact, far from rejoicing at the triumph of conservatism, "a deep-seated pessimism" had taken hold among antiliberal conservatives, and for good reason. From 1988 to 2016—seven consecutive presidential contests—the Republican Party nominated only liberal conservatives. Bush was followed by Robert Dole, the "archetypal stalwart of liberal-Republican support for the welfare state," as Christopher Caldwell described him at the time, and then, four years later, George W. Bush ran on a liberal conservative theme of "compassionate conservatism."[10]

Bush became a bogeyman to liberal Democrats because of the Iraq War and his post-9/11 policies, including the use of torture against suspected terrorists and their detention as noncombatants, without the rights and protections afforded prisoners of war. Bush and Congress also increased the federal government's powers of surveillance of the American population. But, again, these were not the product of Bush's conservatism any more than the repression of Germans, antiwar protesters, and suspected radicals during World War One, or the internment of Japanese American citizens in World War Two, were "conservative." (Even the ACLU did not object to the dreadful denial of civil liberties to Japanese Americans.) The protection of individual rights has always suffered in the United States during times of perceived national crisis, whether the administration was conservative or progressive, Democrat or Republican. Nor is U.S. intervention abroad a "conservative" act, unless Woodrow Wilson, Franklin Roosevelt, Harry Truman, John F. Kennedy, and Bill Clinton were conservatives.

In most other respects, the younger president Bush was among the most liberal Republicans in a century. Tacking away from the conservative assault on "big government," he expanded the federal government's role in education, working with Massachusetts's very liberal Senator Ted Kennedy. Bush sought to expand Medicare to include a prescription-drug benefit. He wanted to expand programs to subsidize minority home ownership. "There is a role for government," he insisted. "We have a responsibility that when somebody hurts, government has got to move."[11] Whether or not he delivered on that responsibility, to say such a thing out loud was anathema to antiliberal conservatives.

On religious matters, Bush was both ecumenical and respectful of America's secular governance. Although he was a born-again Christian, his religiosity, like Jimmy Carter's, was very much in the American liberal tradition. Not only did he make clear that he regarded all religions as equal, including Catholicism, Judaism, and Islam; he made no effort to bring religion into governance. After the 9/11 attacks, he went out of his way to declare Islam a religion of peace and pushed back against the rampant Islamophobia in the country and the Republican Party. On racial issues, he was no less liberal than Bill Clinton. As Gerstle notes, Bush "brought his multiculturalism to the White House," in part by appointing "more minorities to positions requiring Senate confirmation than any Republican president in history," including the first female Black national security adviser, the first *two* Black secretaries of state, and the first Latino attorney general.[12] Bush's posture on racial issues was only the most obvious sign of how far the influence of antiliberalism had fallen in the decades since Buckley and other conservatives openly supported white supremacy in the South. Buckley himself had long since been forced to repudiate his past statements on racial issues, along with many other *National Review* contributors of that era, not to mention dozens of Republican (and Democratic) politicians with Klan memberships or segregationist or white supremacist statements and votes in their past.

On no issue was Bush more at odds with the anti-liberal forces in the Republican Party than immigration. By the beginning of the twenty-first century, the liberal reforms of the Immigration Act of 1965 had once again transformed the American demographic picture. By abolishing the national-origins quotas of the 1920s and replacing them with a preference system based chiefly on an immigrant's family relationships or their possession of desirable skills, the new immigration laws opened the United States to many more immigrants from all over the world. In this third great wave of immigration to the United States, more than fifty-eight million new immigrants arrived in America between 1965 and 2015, compared with eighteen million in the second wave (1890–1919), and fourteen million in the first wave (1840–89). In 1970, the percentage of foreign-born Americans had reached its lowest point since the early nineteenth century, at 4.7 percent. By the 2010s, the percentage was up to almost 14 percent, just shy of the twentieth-century high point of 1910—and with the same effect of stirring powerful currents of white nativism.[13]

For the first time in the nation's history, the overwhelming majority of immigrants did not come from Europe. Out of the fifty-eight million new immigrants,

84 percent came from Latin America, East Asia, South Asia, the Middle East, and Africa, which had a dramatic effect on the complexion of the body politic. The number of legal and illegal immigrants from Mexico alone topped sixteen million, equal to the total number of legal immigrants from Europe between 1890 and the end of World War One. The authors of the 1965 law, who included Ted Kennedy, insisted at the time that it would "not upset the ethnic mix of our society," but it did. In 1965, white people from Europe made up 84 percent of the American population, with Hispanics counting for less than 4 percent and Asians less than 1 percent. By 2015, the white population was down to 62 percent and falling, Hispanics were at 18 percent, and Asians at 6 percent, and rising.[14]

The reaction of many Americans was the same as the reaction following the great influx of Eastern and Southeastern Europeans at the turn of the twentieth century. Californians began to complain that their state was turning into "Mexifornia." All kinds of conservative organizations sprouted up in opposition to immigration, and other groups, like the Tea Party, which took on both the liberal Republican leadership and Obama on a number of issues, were clearly stimulated by the rising immigration numbers.

For antiliberal conservatives, Bush was a particular disaster on the immigration question. In the 2000 Republican primaries, he ran as a pro-immigration candidate. While there was a political calculus in seeking immigrant votes, especially in Bush's native Texas, Bush was genuinely a "multiculturalist." He did not share the common fear of those years, expressed most prominently by Samuel P. Huntington in his 2004 book, *Who Are We?*, that the growth of the Spanish-speaking population endangered the American "Anglo-Protestant" character. Reprising the arguments of 1920s white Protestantism for a modern American audience, Huntington insisted that the principles of the Declaration were the product of the "distinct Anglo-Protestant culture," the key elements of which included "the English language; Christianity; religious commitment; English concepts of the rule of law, the responsibility of rulers, and the rights of individuals; and dissenting Protestant values of individualism, the work ethic, and the belief that humans have the ability and the duty to create a heaven on earth, a 'city on a hill.'" These assertions were wrong on almost every single point, and not least his claim that "Anglo-Protestantism" had been "central to American identity for three centuries. . . ." But he was right to predict the rise of a "white nativist" movement bent on "rebellion" against both the "profound demographic changes" and the demands of multiculturalists.[15]

Bush, in this respect, was an enemy. In a statement that, as Gerstle notes, would have gotten him "tossed out of the GOP" in 2016, Bush declared in his 2000 campaign, "America has had one national creed, but many accents." It had become "one of the largest Spanish-speaking nations in the world"—if one stood in Miami or San Antonio or Los Angeles with eyes closed, "you could just as easily be in Santo Domingo or Santiago." Bush, of course, was in Miami, drumming up Latino votes, when he said that, but he did not have to wear his pro-immigration stance so prominently. "For years our nation has debated this change," he said, and "by nominating me, my party had made a choice to welcome the New America." As president, Bush tried twice to pass immigration reform, which would include a path to citizenship for those immigrants who were in the country illegally, again working with Ted Kennedy, along with John McCain. Meanwhile, resentment against Bush grew among conservatives as he continually "ascribed his opponents' views to nativism or bigotry."[16]

As in the Eisenhower years, antiliberals again came to regard both parties as part of the Eastern elite, urban, liberal consensus and thus equally out of touch with the average white American. Newt Gingrich expressed the general conservative disdain for what he called "the Rockefeller-Bush wing of the party."[17] The Tea Party, born in the early days of the Obama presidency, partly as a response to the financial crisis of 2008 and the bailouts, was notable for its hostility to both parties.[18]

Although the Republican Party continued to nominate liberal conservatives—John McCain in 2008; Mitt Romney in 2012—the ranks of antiliberalism grew increasingly rancorous. The third-party candidacy of Buchanan went nowhere, and such broad-based antiliberal conservative groups as the Klan and the John Birch Society were no longer regarded as respectable even in conservative circles. Although the Republican Party was now the only hope for antiliberals, until 2016 they were locked out of the top ranks of power.

The antiliberal forces were nevertheless growing in the Republican Party, not because the absolute number of antiliberals in the country was growing—it may even have been diminishing—but because by the 2000s the Republican Party pretty much had them all. Indeed, an interesting and, as it would turn out, fateful dynamic had been occurring in American politics. The core antiliberal constituencies were declining in absolute numbers in the country at large, but as a percentage of Republicans, they were growing in both numbers and influence.

This was a gradual process. As late as the Reagan years, there had still been a substantial Southern white constituency in the Democratic Party, but over the course of the 1990s and into the 2000s, many Southern Democrats migrated to the Republican Party, leaving the Democratic Party all but purged of antiliberal racist elements. Christopher Caldwell at the time lamented the Republican Party's slide into "southern captivity." The Republicans won House majorities in 1994 and 1996 largely by picking up some two dozen seats in the South, while Republican representation in liberal New England all but disappeared. The Republican congressional leadership by the late 1990s, led in the House by Newt Gingrich of Georgia and Dick Armey and Tom DeLay of Texas, was overwhelmingly from the South. As Caldwell correctly observed, the more the Republican Party became the party of the South, the more it tended to drive liberals, moderates, and even other conservatives from other regions out of the party.[19] This was all part of the great national re-sorting that occurred throughout the last decades of the twentieth century and into the twenty-first. The modern Democratic Party, once the party of slaveholders and Jim Crow, became increasingly the party of minorities, women, and other groups who wanted to see rights expanded, and the Republican Party, once the party of Lincoln, increasingly became the party of white males, eager to hold on to their primacy in American society.

Another important shift was among more and less educated voters. As late as 1992, some 50 percent of white voters without a college degree identified as Democrats, while 41 percent identified as Republicans. By 2016, those numbers had flipped, with Republicans getting 59 percent of non-college-educated voters to the Democrats' 33 percent. But at the same time, the percentage of the overall population with no college degree was declining. Here, too, a shrinking bloc of white conservative voters was increasing its influence in the Republican Party.[20]

By the 2000s, the Republican Party had effectively become an ingathering of antiliberalism in America, which swelled its percentage of the party and made it harder for Republican leaders to ignore and suppress. As with other such demographic trends, the political effect of this movement was delayed. In 2000, Republicans chose George W. Bush with 60 percent of the primary vote; John McCain was second with 32 percent; and there was no antiliberal conservative candidate to speak of. In 2008, John McCain won 47 percent of the Republican primary vote, and his two closest challengers were Mitt Romney (21 percent) and Mike Huckabee (20 percent, the only antiliberal conservative in the race). But a striking change was visible in the 2012 primaries. Romney won 52 percent of the primary vote, but the next-highest vote getters were Rick Santorum (20 percent), Newt Gingrich (14 percent), and Ron Paul (10 percent), all of whom were antiliberal conservative leaders. That was 44 percent of Republican primary voters, almost exactly the percentage that would vote for Trump in the 2016 primaries. Indeed, Trump himself toyed with running that year, and might have won the nomination in 2012 had he stayed in the race. At the time when he dropped out, to return to his successful television program, he was leading Romney in the polls. By 2016, antiliberalism had become dominant, at least in the Republican primaries. In addition to Trump's 44 percent, another antiliberal candidate, Ted Cruz, picked up 25-percent support. Those regarded as the leading "establishment" conservative candidates in 2016, liberal conservatives all, received just 26 percent—Marco Rubio (11 percent), John Kasich (14 percent), and Jeb Bush (1 percent). Even if they had not divided the establishment Republican vote among themselves, they would not have defeated the antiliberal candidate.

What happened between 2008 and 2016 that unseated the liberal conservative leadership of the Republican Party and turned it into the party of the Trump movement? Many believe it was the financial crisis of 2008 and the deep recession that followed, but polling studies show that the biggest reason was the election of the first Black president in American history. Though Black people and many millions of white Americans rejoiced at this remarkable occurrence, there were, predictably, many millions of white voters who did not. The Tea Party movement that arose during Obama's first year in office included several strains of American antiliberalism: religious conservatives who opposed Obama's Affordable Care Act because it covered abortions; others who opposed "big government" in general; and those who worried about excessive government spending and opposed the Bush and Obama administrations' bank and industry bailouts. But there was no missing the white supremacist attitudes that united them all, which combined long-developing anti-immigrant sentiments with hostility to the very idea of a Black president, never mind a liberal Democratic Black president whose father (whom Obama barely knew) was reportedly a Kenyan anticolonial Marxist.

Suddenly, an open racism not seen in decades re-emerged. As Obama himself later observed, "It was as if my very presence in the White House had triggered a deep-seated panic, a sense that the natural order had been disrupted."[21] The Tea Party's most famous spokesman at the time, the Fox News star Glenn Beck, told his audience that Obama has "exposed himself as a guy, over and over and over again, who has a deep-seated hatred for white people or the white culture." The former House Speaker Newt Gingrich argued that Obama's behavior was "so outside our comprehension" that it made sense "only if you understand Kenyan, anti-colonial behavior."[22]

Conservative social media posted pictures depicting Obama as a monkey and as an African witch doctor with a bone through his nose. Tea Party demonstrators held signs that read "OBAMANOMICS: MONKEY SEE, MONKEY SPEND" and "CONGRESS = SLAVE OWNER; TAXPAYER = NIGGAR [*sic*]." At one point in Obama's first term, a crowd of Tea Party demonstrators surrounded two Black members of Congress—one of them was the 1960s civil rights activist John Lewis—and chanted at them: "Nigger! Nig-ger!"[23] When they weren't accusing Obama of being an anti-American Marxist African anticolonialist, they accused him of being a Muslim. Inevitably, some conspiracists circulated the accusation that Obama was not an American at all. The "birther" movement grew in popularity to the point where an aspiring Republican presidential candidate, Donald Trump, made it his debut issue in 2012.

Then there was the continuing question of immigration. After Mitt Romney's defeat and Obama's reelection in 2012, the Republican Party leadership produced an "autopsy" to explain the loss and propose changes to lift the party's fortunes—Republicans had by then lost two consecutive elections to Obama and had lost the popular vote in every election except one since 1992. The answer seemed obvious to the party's establishment: the nation's demographic changes required an adjustment. Republicans could not continue to be only the party of white men, if only because white men were a shrinking percentage of the voting population. Bush in his two successful elections had won a substantial portion of the Hispanic vote, largely on the basis of his pro-immigration stance and warmth toward the Spanish-speaking community in America. McCain, offering "a little straight talk," said, "Republicans have got to compete for the Hispanic voter." South Carolina's senator Lindsey Graham declared 2013 "the year of immigration reform." America, he said, "is an idea; nobody owns it."[24] The so-called Gang of Eight, which included four senators from each party, including past and future Republican candidates McCain and Marco Rubio, put together a plan to put millions of undocumented immigrants on a path to citizenship, allowing them to work legally and reunite with family members. The Senate overwhelmingly approved the bill, in a remarkable display of bipartisan comity on such an explosive issue. But the explosion occurred in the House, where Republicans refused to take it up, despite then Speaker John Boehner's efforts to move it.

This was the first significant sign of the brewing anti-liberal rebellion in the Republican Party. Some conservative Republicans, in fact, drew the opposite conclusion from the party's 2012 "autopsy." Instead of wanting to expand to include more people of color, especially Latinos but also Black people, these conservatives aimed to boost turnout of their core constituency: white people. Instead of "outreach," they called for "in-reach" aimed at the "missing white voters" who they rightly believed had sat out the 2012 election or had even voted for Obama, so uninspired were they by the liberal conservative Romney.[25] In practice, this meant playing on white fears that their culture was being overtaken by non-white, non-American alien invaders and that white people in general faced "replacement" by non-white people, including Jews.

The latter half of the Obama presidency saw a series of racial and cultural collisions of the kind that had always produced potent antiliberal uprisings and that gave antiliberal conservatives the kindling to start another national brush fire. Racial tensions reached a high pitch following several prominent shootings of young Black men, some by white vigilantes under the guise of self-protection, as with the murder of Trayvon Martin in Florida in February 2012, and many others by police. The police shooting of a Black teen in Ferguson, Missouri, in August 2014 led to massive protests across the country, and the broad national expansion of the Black Lives Matter movement, which had begun after the killing of Martin. Many Americans who had hoped and assumed that time and the civil rights victories of the 1960s had reduced the levels of prejudice and discrimination in the country were horrified to "learn" that Black people were, in fact, still treated very differently from white people, by both the police and the legal system. Many were also troubled to learn that a good portion of their fellow white people were uninterested in this and preferred to regard Black people themselves as the problem. In the summer of 2016, in the middle of the general election campaign, Black NFL players began taking a knee during the playing of the national anthem to protest the treatment of Black people by police across the country, which infuriated many of the white fans, who saw it as an insult to the country and to those who died defending it. The issues had shifted—racial tensions were no longer about Jim Crow laws but about an unspoken but pervasive discrimination with often deadly consequences—but the divisions they aroused were strikingly similar.

Another critical moment came with the Supreme Court's decision in the summer of 2015 to legalize same-sex marriages, compelling local officials to grant marriage licenses to gay couples. Public opinion had shifted rapidly: in 2009, polls showed Americans opposed same-sex marriage by 54 to 37 percent; by 2015, when the court handed down its decision, Americans *favored* same-sex marriage by the same margin, 55 to 39. Even among Republicans, support went from 21 percent in 2009 to 38 percent in 2015.[26] Nevertheless, the Supreme Court's declaration that same-sex marriage was protected by the

Constitution inevitably infuriated religious conservatives already upset about the expanding government support for abortion, as well as the shifting place of women in society. For decades, Christian leaders like Jerry Falwell had been warning that "the present moral crisis" over homosexuality was part of a broader crisis of modern, secular America in which both men and women no longer "accepted their proper roles as designated by God"—i.e., "for men to be manly and spiritual" and for women to be "feminine" and "submissive." Homosexuality was "Satan's diabolical attack upon the family, God's order in Creation."[27]

Once again, the court had done nothing more than acknowledge the rights of a group previously discriminated against for reasons of religion and tradition. The court was not creating new rights; it was applying liberal principles to circumstances the founders had not envisioned. The idea of gay marriage was almost unimaginable in the eighteenth century, just as women's equality had also been unimaginable to the overwhelming majority of Americans. It took time for people to realize that the prohibitions against gay marriage violated the liberal principles of the Declaration just as the prohibitions on Black people's full participation in American society did. The Reagan appointee Anthony Kennedy grounded the majority's decision in the natural-rights liberalism of the revolutionary era and the early republic.

Although not as significant as the abolition of prayer in public schools, which still infuriated religious conservatives, or the court's 1973 decision declaring a woman's right to abortion, the decision on gay marriage set off powerful protests by an increasingly vocal and antiliberal "Christian nationalist" movement.

"Christian nationalism" was nothing new in the United States, of course. Despite the founders' clear views on the separation of church and state, many Americans had always believed that America was part of God's plan and that the founders themselves meant to establish a Christian nation. That view is widely shared in the United States today. According to a Pew survey in October 2022, 60 percent of Americans believe that the founders "originally intended" the United States to be a "Christian nation"; 45 percent believe that the United States "should be" a Christian nation; and fully a third believe the United States is "now" a Christian nation.[28] As Robert Jeffress, the Southern Baptist televangelist and pastor of a Dallas megachurch, put it, "America was founded predominantly . . . by Christians who wanted to build a Christian nation on the foundations of God's will."[29]

This belief can take a mild or an extreme form. In recent years, more extreme versions of Christian nationalism have emerged to wield significant influence in the political system. A significant driving force in Christian nationalism in recent decades, for instance, has been the Christian Reconstruction or "Dominionist" theological movement. Derived chiefly from a Dutch Reformed version of Calvinism, as well as from the nineteenth-century Southern Baptist theologian Robert Lewis Dabney, this theological doctrine holds that Christ's "dominion" covers every aspect of life, from the private to the political. As the early-twentieth-century neo-Calvinist theologian Abraham Kuyper put it, "There is not a square inch in the whole domain of our human existence over which Christ, who is Sovereign over all, does not cry, Mine!"[30]

From the beginning, in America at least, this doctrine has been closely associated with white supremacy. Dabney, writing at the dawn of the Jim Crow era, was a leading promoter of the biblical justification for slavery, still arguing more than two decades after the Civil War that "the relation of master and bondman was sanctified by the administration of a divine sacrament."[31] His blending of Calvinist theology and white supremacy left a powerful legacy. The Christian nationalist theologian R. J. Rushdoony, who popularized Dominionism for a modern American audience in the late 1960s and early '70s, also insisted that the founders had aimed to "perpetuate a Christian order" through the Constitution. He claimed that the Fourteenth Amendment, granting equal citizenship to Black people, began a retreat from that earlier "conception of America as a Christian country." Insisting that only biblical law was the true law, and, contrary to the founders, that human reason was incapable of discovering the truth, he argued that it was the task of Christians to "reconstruct" civilization to establish Christ's "dominion" over all things—"one faith, one law and one standard of justice." He opposed democracy as a "heresy" and argued that Christianity and democracy were "inevitably enemies."[32]

Today, Dominionism has lodged itself firmly in the Republican Party. In Texas and other states, wealthy donors back candidates who endorse Dominionist positions on public school education and other issues and oppose candidates who do not. The Missouri senator Josh Hawley quotes Kuyper and articulates Dominionist theology, and he is open about his antiliberalism. America is a "revolutionary nation," he insists, not because of the principles of the Declaration but "because we are the heirs of the revolution of the Bible" that began with "the founding of the nation of Israel."[33] There could hardly be a statement more at odds with the American founders' liberal, ecumenical vision, but tens of millions of Americans agree.

That, of course, was not what the founders wanted, but it is what many Christian nationalists do want. They want a different type of nation, and from their perspective they are right. The American system that the founders created will not allow them to achieve their theological objectives.

Critics of liberalism are right to point out that the rights-protection machine that the founders set in motion is destructive of many traditions, and that includes religious institutions. It exerts pressure on all hierarchies and belief systems that limit the freedom of individuals to think and act as they please. Liberalism, for instance, *has* been destructive of the traditional patriarchal hierarchy of the family. By granting women equal rights both in and out of the home, liberalism has weakened the "dominion" of men. It has changed the nature of marriage and in some ways even the definition and understanding of what marriage is for. So, of course, has technology, in the form of contraceptives and abortion, but it is liberalism that allowed women to take advantage of that technology, freeing them to play roles that were once played only by men. Hierarchy lies at the heart of traditional Christianity in both its Catholic and Protestant variations. There is God, the father of creation; then the Pope or divinely chosen king, the father of the church or realm; then the father as head of the family. That is the proper Christian order of things, and the slave was also part of this divinely ordained hierarchy. That is what many American Christians have always believed, and they have viewed liberalism, correctly, as a threat to those hierarchies. Traditional religions have also tended to demand participation by the entire society, not just pockets of believers. The idea of many religions coexisting under the umbrella of a secular government and society was invented by the United States and had previously existed nowhere else in history. The Ottomans tolerated other religions but severely constrained the public practice of any religion except Islam; the Roman Catholic Church allowed no heresies. Calvin's Geneva was a totalitarian theocracy much like modern Iran, and until the eighteenth century, governments in Protestant countries always insisted on the primacy of Protestantism and discriminated against other denominations, and that included prerevolutionary America. The early Puritans were typical in believing that personal salvation required living in a "godly" Christian society; it was vitally important not only to be pious but to make sure that one's neighbors and community were also pious, lest God visit His wrath on all. Today, many evangelical Christians are content to try to live godly lives in this liberal secular society without demanding that everyone else do so, too. But there is also a large number of people who believe that the United States either is or should be a "Christian nation" and want the federal government to reflect that. In this critical respect, they are antiliberal, and they cannot achieve their ends without fundamentally changing the nature of the American system.

White Christians and many others in the antiliberal coalition insist that it is they who are oppressed. It is they who have been deprived of their freedom. And, in a sense, they are right, if by "freedom" they mean their ability to demand that others bow to their hierarchies. The slaveholders insisted they were deprived of their "freedom" to hold human beings as property; Southerners in the post-Reconstruction era insisted on their "freedom" to oppress Black citizens in their states. Today, antiliberals in American society are indeed deprived of their "freedom" to impose their views on society. American society was founded on liberal principles, with institutions established specifically to safeguard and promote liberalism, including public school systems that inculcate liberal values among students. The antiliberal political theorist Patrick Deneen calls this "liberal totalitarianism."[34] The Christian in America, Rushdoony complained, "has no right to his identity; he must recognize all others and their 'rights,' but he himself has none."[35] This is true if a Christian's "rights" include the right not only to lead a Christian life himself but to impose that life on the entire society. What Christian nationalists call "liberal totalitarianism" the founders called "freedom of conscience."

This is not a new complaint spurred by some recent radical leftward turn in American politics. Rushdoony was complaining about the oppressions of white people and Christians almost six decades ago, long before the onset of what conservative Americans call "wokeness." He was responding not to "woke" corporations or Black Lives Matter but to the civil rights legislation of the 1950s and '60s. Then, too, it seems, the "white man" was being "systematically indoctrinated into believing he is guilty of enslaving and abusing the Negro" (when, in fact, Rushdoony insisted, "nowhere in all history or in the world today has the Negro been better off" than in the United States, including under slavery).[36] The current conservative outrage at American-history curricula that acknowledge the systemic racism which has shaped that history is not new. Nor is it new that many white people feel that the demands of minority groups for both rights and respect have "gone too far." In the 1960s, surveys taken by *The New York Times* showed that majorities of white people believed even then that the Civil Rights Movement had "gone too far," that Black people were receiving "everything on a silver platter" and the government was practicing "reverse discrimination" against white people.[37] Liberalism is always going too far for many Americans, and certainly for antiliberals.

Today, the main target of antiliberal conservatism is "wokeness." But what is "wokeness"? To some extent, it is the inevitable by-product of the liberal system the founders created. When groups that have been struggling for recognition of their fundamental natural rights finally succeed, they invariably seek more than just acknowledgment of those rights. They seek the respect and dignity that come with being fully equal members of society, no more or less privileged than those who used to oppress and look down on them and diminish them with disparaging language and stereotypes. Not only did Jews, Italians, and Irish want to be treated as equals under the law; they wanted to be treated as equals in society. They did not want to be the targets of ethnic slurs, and they also did not want to be ridiculed and stereotyped in the popular discourse as greedy Shylocks, mafiosi, and drunkards. And society was gradually compelled to conform, so that today it is regarded as unacceptable to use such words or such stereotypes in public or in what used to be called "polite company."

Today's "wokeness" is the same, only now it is other groups demanding respect. Any sixty-five-year-old white, heterosexual male knows that he grew up using language and thinking about Black people, women, gay people, and other non-white people and nonheterosexuals in ways that today are widely and correctly regarded as unacceptable. At the time, people were often scarcely aware that what they were saying or thinking could be regarded as offensive, in part because Black people, women, gay people, and other minorities were still fighting over more fundamental issues. But once having gained a measure of legal and institutional equality, like the ethnic immigrants and other minority groups that preceded them, they wanted to be treated with the respect in society that

equals deserved, and fully included in the big and growing American family.

Many people assume that laws change as social customs and mores change, and sometimes that is true.
But the relationship between the requirements of liberalism and social mores is more dynamic than that.
Social mores change because groups of people who are
discriminated against demand their rights and appeal to
the principles of the founders to justify their demands.
When the courts determine that a group has indeed
been unfairly discriminated against, members of the
group demand not only that their rights be respected
but also that society adjust and adapt to the fact of
their equality. That is when social mores and customs
change, and often to the frustration of those forced to
adapt. Today once-privileged groups chafe at having to
adjust their language and ways of thinking to the latest
assimilation of once-despised groups. No doubt many
early-twentieth-century American Protestants were also
annoyed at having to bite their tongues before uttering a
disparaging comment about the Irish Catholics and Jews
in their midst.

Yes, "wokeness" can be and has been carried to excess,
and there does come a point where the legitimate desire
to insist on inoffensive speech and behavior conflicts
with the vital liberal values of free speech and free
thought. The American academy has been badly dam-

aged by rampant ideological intolerance and by the faculties' assaults on liberalism itself as somehow being the cause of the nation's ills rather than the answer. When students refuse to let a dissenting or even offensive speaker speak, they are denying free speech with bullying force. At that point, "wokeness" becomes antiliberal, too. But most of the demand for "wokeness" today—as was true a century ago, when demanded by a different set of minorities—is the unavoidable consequence of a liberal system and its accompanying egalitarian spirit.

Antiliberals may complain about wokeness, therefore, but it is the liberal system of government bequeathed by the founders that they are really objecting to. What they seek is the overthrow of the liberal foundations of American society. What they really want, as Deneen frankly proclaims, is "regime change."

Since the birth of the American republic, many American citizens have tolerated the system only for as long as they were allowed to ignore it and keep liberalism at bay, as long as they were allowed to maintain their preliberal traditions. But whenever pressure to conform to the nation's liberal principles has grown, millions of Americans have pushed back, resisted, and fought to retain their antiliberal ways. And when the time came when they could resist no longer, they have sought escape.

6

The Rebellion

TODAY, THE FORCES of antiliberalism can see that time, demographics, and the system are all working against them. The complexion of the country has changed too much. White supremacy as a political platform is losing viability as the white population dwindles. Their only option, as antiliberal intellectuals like Deneen and legal scholar Adrian Vermeule argue, is to overthrow the system, now, in the 2024 election.

Antiliberals these days talk openly about overthrowing the system or undermining it from within. Abandoned by a Republican Party that "does not really care about them" and by a "conservative establishment" that has made its peace with "the progressive project of narcotizing the American people and turning us into a nation of slaves," antiliberals "must tremble indefinitely under the axe," writes one conservative scholar. Unless they take dramatic action, the "victory of progressive tyranny will be assured. See you in the gulag."[1]

These antiliberals candidly call for freeing the nation from the founders' liberal vision. The founders' legacy is a "dead end," writes Glenn Ellmers, a scholar at the Claremont Institute. The Constitution is a "Potemkin village"; elections, "even if conducted legitimately," no longer "reflect the will of the people" but resemble elections in the "communist regimes of the 20th century." Indeed, Ellmers argues, reflecting the antiliberal tradition in its most basic form, "most people living in the United States today—certainly more than half—are not Americans in any meaningful sense of the term." They are "zombie[s]" and "human rodent[s]" who live "a shadow-life of timid conformity." Only "the 75 million people who voted in the last election" for Trump are true "Americans." The United States, he argues, "has become two nations occupying the same country." Instead of trying to compete with Democrats in elections that don't reflect the will of the people, Ellmers writes, "why not just cut to the chase and skip the empty, meaningless process?" The "only road forward" is overthrowing "the existing post-American order."[2]

And replace it with what? The goal, antiliberals insist, is a society and a political system dedicated to the "common good." What they mean is a Christian commonwealth: a "culture that preserves and encourages order and continuity, and support for religious belief and institutions," with legislation to "promote public morality, and forbid its intentional corruption," a "forthright acknowledgment and renewal of the Christian roots of our civilization," "public opportunities for prayers," and a "revitalization of our public spaces to reflect a deeper belief that we are called to erect imitations of the beauty that awaits us in another Kingdom."[3]

None of these antiliberal intellectuals, some of whom are Catholics, explain which version of Christianity the government under their leadership will promote. Apparently, they are confident that the five-century struggle between Protestants and Catholics over Christian doctrine has been forever amicably settled. It does not seem to occur to them that the reason they can even contemplate a "Christian" nation without the deadly doctrinal disputes that have marked Christianity for two millennia is that American liberalism has over the course of two centuries forced these different sects of Christianity to coexist, along with Jews, Muslims, and numerous other religions and religious sects. But if these Christian nationalists have their way and replace America's liberal society with a government directing people to the "common good," it is not clear how they will avoid returning to the doctrinal disputes over what the "common good" means, disagreements over which Christians slaughtered one another for centuries. Never mind what happens to non-Christians in the Christian commonwealth that antiliberals seek to create. Antiliberals may use the term "Judeo-Christian" all they like, but if the past is any guide, it will not be Jews, or Muslims, or probably even Catholics who determine what the new government-approved and supported religious institutions of a "post-liberal" America will look like.

And what about white people? Do even white Protestants agree on what constitutes the "common good"? Will they simply live in harmony once the non-white people have been put back in their place or removed and "wokeness" is suppressed by the government? The history of Europe should dispel such fancies. White people have historically no more agreed on the "common good" than Christians. Americans used to regard it as a matter of pride that peoples who fought one another for centuries in Europe could live together peacefully in America. That was the consequence of a liberal society in which all enjoyed equal rights. But history amply shows that this is not the normal condition of humans. It is utopian to imagine that, in the absence of the institutions and safeguards of liberalism to constrain them, these ancient divisions will not reemerge.

Antiliberal intellectuals don't trouble themselves with such matters. The founders labored to create something that could last. The antiliberals want to destroy what the founders created but lack a coherent plan for what could replace it. Their goal is destruction and revenge. Trump for these intellectuals is an imperfect if essential vehicle for counterrevolution. A "deeply flawed narcissist" suffering from a "bombastic vanity," he has "lacked the discipline to target his creative/destructive tendencies effectively." His movement remains "untutored and ill led." Trump's failure to execute the counterrevolution in his first term was a failure to develop "a capable leadership class," but antiliberal intellectuals have the answer: them. They hope to use the rebellious destructiveness of the Trump movement to overthrow a liberal "elite," against which they have been helpless by themselves, and replace it with another "elite"—a "self-conscious aristoi," Deneen calls it, who understand "both the disease afflicting the nation, and the revolutionary medicine required for the cure," who know how to turn populist "resentments into sustained policy." Like Lenin, this new would-be elite yearns to place itself at the vanguard of the populist revolution, acting "on behalf of the broad working class" while raising the consciousness of the "untutored" masses.[4] Indeed, according to the prominent antiliberal Harvard law professor Adrian Vermeule, it will be necessary to impose the "common good" even against the people's "own perceptions of what is best for them"—a most Leninist concept indeed.

Clearly, the new antiliberal government will not be a democracy. It will be an antiliberal tyranny. The new state, Vermeule writes, with its "robust executive," will "sear the liberal faith with hot irons," wielding the "authority to curb the social and economic pretensions of the urban-gentry liberals."[5] The whiff of violence and oppression in such statements is intentional. The antiliberal intellectuals understand that to change the liberal system will require more than legislative reforms. The founders, despite everything, did manage to erect a system that was capable of defending itself against antiliberal rebellion from within. To those who feel oppressed by liberalism, the only answer is to overthrow the system and the Constitution that undergirds it.

For the first time since the Civil War, antiliberals have the means to do so. The antiliberal takeover of the Republican Party since Trump won the party's nomination in 2016 threatens American liberal democracy in a way that the founders neither envisioned nor prepared defenses against. The two-party system, which the founders did not foresee, has served many useful purposes. But it has also turned out to be the trapdoor through which tyranny can sneak in and destroy democracy.

When the founders established the checks and balances to ensure against the rise of a tyrannical demagogue, they did not envision national parties uniting broad coalitions of interregional interests. The world they lived in was centered on the states; it was more a confederation of independent countries than a unified nation. Regional differences seemed as enormous as the vast distances that separated them in the days before motorized transportation; the needs of the growing West were radically different from the needs of the Northeast and the South. The idea that a national party could speak for all those disparate state and regional interests seemed unlikely. Nor did they imagine that a single demagogue could gain a national following, for much the same reason.

The founders also hoped that the checks and balances they established in the Constitution would be sufficient to contain the ambitions of a demagogue. But this assumption rested on a further expectation: that the three branches of government—Congress, the executive, and the judiciary—would jealously guard their institutional prerogatives. For most of the country's history, this has held true. Even when Congress was controlled by the president's party, congressional leaders resisted executive encroachments on the legislature's constitutional authority. But today party unity trumps interbranch rivalry. Party leaders in Congress increasingly do as their presidents bid them. Certainly, this Republican Party has become subservient to one man and his national following. Neither a Republican-dominated Congress nor even the Republican-dominated Supreme Court can be counted on to assert independent authority if the interests of the Trump-led party are at stake.

Indeed, antiliberalism has once again found a home in the Supreme Court. In the middle of the nineteenth century, the court backed slavery, and not just because it was protected in the Constitution but because justices agreed with the majority view that Black people were not equal to white people. Then, for almost a century after Reconstruction, the court effectively endorsed official segregation and Jim Crow laws. Today much of the court has adopted an "originalism" that is inherently antiliberal, because it seeks to treat eighteenth-century practices and traditions as a guide to what is constitutional, rather than the liberal principles the founders promulgated knowing full well that they were at odds with Americans' practices and traditions at the time. Between the court's increasingly antiliberal bent and its oft-demonstrated partisanship (the partisan 5–4 decision in *Bush v. Gore* in 2000 being a prime example), it may prove a thin reed to rely on if and when an electoral and constitutional crisis erupts.

7

Trump, Savior and Destroyer

DONALD TRUMP MIGHT seem an odd choice to lead the greatest rebellion against the American liberal constitutional order since the Civil War. He certainly had no such grand ambitions when he first ran for office. Indeed, given Trump's unquestionable place as one of the most significant figures in American history, it is remarkable how petty and trivial his ambitions really were. He ran for president on a lark, more as a business and branding venture than out of interest in actually being president. He believed he had no more than a 10-percent chance of winning when he first ran. He had no program—he worked out his first campaign platform with Roger Stone—and no commitment to any particular set of policies. Over his decades in public life, he had veered back and forth between liberal and conservative positions, and also between the two parties. Such shiftiness is not unusual for politicians, but he was not even consistently a politician. He was first and foremost a businessman, consistent only in his desire to make money, expand the Trump brand, and serve his own ego. Even his closest advisers and supporters never doubted that his interests were entirely selfish. Yet his uncanny ability to appeal to a certain type of voter gave him a unique charisma for many Americans.

The nature of that appeal was clear from the beginning: Trump made himself the leading spokesman and defender of white Christian supremacy in America. In his abortive 2012 campaign, the issue Trump chose to focus on more than any other, the issue with which he made his name synonymous, was the birther conspiracy. In his debut before the Conservative Political Action Conference in February 2011, he declared, "Our current president came out of nowhere. . . . The people who went to school with him, they never saw him—they don't know who he is." Maybe Obama was a Muslim, Trump suggested: "I don't know." Even Roger Stone warned him that the "established media" were going to "destroy" him for "race-baiting."[1] But as Trump hammered on the theme—aided by Sean Hannity at Fox News, who aired segments on Obama's birth practically every day through the month of April 2011—Trump's poll numbers rose. He led all Republican candidates before dropping out of the race to return to his hit TV show, *The Apprentice*.

When he ran again in 2016, his identity as a white male supremacist was well established, therefore, and it paid off. And not just with the white working class. Though conventional wisdom sees Trump's movement as that of lower-income, working-class, non-college-educated Americans, a survey of Trump voters by the Pew Research Center following the 2016 election showed that Trump voters were distributed evenly across income levels. In fact, the lowest-income voters cast a majority of votes for Hillary Clinton, and the two candidates virtually tied among voters earning over a hundred thousand dollars a year. The issue that carried Trump was race, not economics. Of those voters who said in exit polls that the economy was the most important issue, Clinton won by 11 points, 52 to 41. Of those who said immigration was the most important issue, Trump won by 31 points, 64 to 33.[2] All white groups voted in greater numbers for Trump in 2016 than they had for Bush in 2000: the white working class, white evangelicals, white Catholics, and white Protestants; white men and white women. One of the biggest jumps in the Republican vote in 2016 was indeed among white people with no college education—Bush won 56 percent of this group in 2000; Trump won 66 percent in 2016. But non-white voters without a college degree voted overwhelmingly for Clinton, 76 to 20. The key variable was race, not education level.

Trump's success among white voters of all classes was, of course, the culmination of a long-term trend—a declining percentage of white voters in the overall electorate, voting increasingly for Republicans. In the 2000 election, white people made up 81 percent of the vote, and Bush beat Al Gore among white voters by 13 points, 55 to 42, while garnering 35 percent of the Hispanic vote and 41 percent of the Asian vote. But by 2012, the white vote was down to 72 percent of the total votes cast, and Romney beat Obama by 20 points among white voters, 59 to 39. In 2016, the white vote was down to 70 percent, with Trump winning among white people again by 20 points, 59 to 39. Though he lost to Biden in 2020, Trump still won by 17 points among white voters, 58 to 41, but the white percentage of the total vote was down to 67, a drop of 14 percentage points from 2000, while the combined vote of non-white people—African Americans, Hispanic Americans, and Asian Americans—rose from 19 to 30 percent.[3]

Trump did bring out the "missing white voters," therefore, and at all income and education levels. He did so not by promising economic or social-welfare programs to address their many material problems but by appealing to their concerns about the declining influence of white culture in America. That was what Making America Great Again meant; it meant restoring white cultural and political primacy.[4] Trump was the answer for white voters unhappy about decades of expanding liberal hegemony and what they regarded as the bullying oppression of the liberal media and government bureaucracy. Trump was *their* bully. Precisely because he was not a politician but a supposedly rich and successful businessman, he could not be controlled by any establishment, even that of the Republican Party. Other antiliberal champions had either been chewed up by the dominant liberal media or, like Newt Gingrich and Ted Cruz, seemed to be playing the usual political games, and not very successfully.

Indeed, the fact that Trump was anything but a good Republican or even a good Christian, but was a crude New York street fighter who flouted all conventions, both liberal and conservative, made him all the more attractive to antiliberal conservatives of all stripes. People knew what they were getting even before he began his run. His persona for eleven successful seasons on *The Apprentice* was as the tough, no-nonsense businessman who said what he thought and wasn't too concerned with the niceties of the modern workplace. His trademark slogan, "You're fired!," showed just enough alpha-male brutality and appealed to many people tired of the politically correct politesse demanded of public figures. This was the guy to take on the dominant liberal coastal "elite." As Norman Podhoretz put it, Trump, "with all his vices," had "the necessary virtues and strength to fight the fight that needs to be fought."[5] The fact that the first prominent thing he chose to focus his campaign on in 2012 was a racist meme alerted everyone to the targets at which his bullying personality would be pointed. That was all Christian conservatives, white supremacists, conservative antiliberal intellectuals, and other parts of the antiliberal coalition needed to know to embrace him as their savior.

Trump's supporters see him as David to the liberal establishment's Goliath. Trump voters in focus groups often say that what they appreciate about him most is his fearlessness in taking on the liberal establishment. Where other Republicans bow and scrape to the liberal media, or are simply destroyed by it, Trump flouts the liberal conventions and gives as good as he gets. Images of Trump as a muscle-bound Superman or Rambo are common, the lone hero in a lopsided battle, taking all the blows the liberals can mete out and still pressing on. When Trump declared in his 2016 campaign, "I am an outsider fighting for you," they believed him. When Trump says, "They are coming after me because I am fighting for you," that is exactly what his supporters believe. When Trump says, "I am your retribution," they thrill at the prospect of the revenge against the liberal "elite" that he promises to carry out once he is back in office.

Trump's hold on the imaginations of millions of Americans is extraordinary. Rarely in American history has a political figure drawn such adoration and complete loyalty while still alive and politically active. Even the revered Reagan was frequently attacked by conservatives for falling short of their expectations. Trump's supporters never criticize him or tolerate criticism of him, even on issues on which they disagree with him. The conservative rebellion against Covid lockdowns and vaccinations during Trump's term in office, for instance, was not driven primarily by paranoia about the government and vaccines. After all, it was their government in charge; it was the vaccine that the Trump administration had approved and worked to produce as quickly as possible. Rather, it was Trump's critics whom they reviled. Trump said the virus would be minor and would pass quickly, and his supporters not only believed him but came up with "proof" that he was right. They turned against Anthony Fauci and the country's health officials because their statements contradicted and embarrassed their hero and leader. A famous conservative law professor at New York University, Richard Epstein, was so slavishly loyal to Trump that he insisted at the beginning of Covid that the virus would cost no more than five hundred lives. (As of November 1, 2023, the number of Covid deaths according to the Centers for Disease Control and Prevention was 1,150,119.) Some Trump supporters who contracted Covid would not even go to the hospital or report that they had the virus, lest they strengthen the liberal critics' case against Trump. "I'm not going to add to the numbers," one Trump supporter told a reporter.[6] A significant number of Trump supporters were prepared to risk death rather than take an action that Trump's critics recommended.

How many politicians could count on such devotion? The daughter of one of the men convicted for his role in the January 6 attack on the Capitol later recalled that when Trump spoke, her father "fell to his knees."[7] How many have movements of voters who travel the country like Deadheads to attend as many Trump rallies as possible, events that stir the emotions to a high pitch, like a nineteenth-century revival meeting or a Beatles concert? As one participant described the typical Trump rally: "The whole place is erupting, everyone is screaming, and your heart is beating like, just, oh my God. It's like nothing I've experienced in my lifetime." Trump gives voice to their anxieties and their anger, but, more than that, he encourages them to have their own voice, to act rather than wallow in victimhood, to celebrate their common hostility to the liberal system.[8] The result is that tens of millions of Americans will follow Trump wherever he leads, including to overthrow a system of government that they no longer value and have come to regard as inimical to their interests.

People are wisely reluctant to throw words like "fascism" around loosely, but it is hard to find a better word for the relationship between Trump the leader and his devoted following. Fascism is the malady to which modern democracies are particularly susceptible, and in an age of mass politics—the age we have been living in for the better part of the last two centuries—various forms of fascism have been the likeliest alternative to democracy. Modern nations are not about to establish monarchies. To have any legitimacy beyond the exercise of brute force, modern leaders must at least appear to speak for the masses. In democracies, they must create mass followings that allow them to win within the democratic system and then transform it into a system they can dominate. Hitler came to power in Germany first by winning democratic elections, by inspiring loyalty among normal middle-class Germans, by offering an alternative to the messy and often gridlocked democracy of Weimar Germany. Only then did he cement his position in power by doing away with democratic forms.

Trump's appeal to the masses propelled him into a position of national power that he barely sought. But, once having gained it, he has not been willing to give it up. His narcissism became megalomania, which in turn has made him a would-be tyrant. This is another one of those accidents, the contingent events that change the course of history. That a man with Trump's personal qualities should run for president just at the time when the strength and fury of American antiliberalism was reaching a new peak will be treated by historians as of a piece and inevitable. But Trump was not inevitable.

What was inevitable was the clash between liberalism and antiliberalism. It was inevitable because it has never ceased.

It took Hitler nine years, from his failed putsch in 1923 to his electoral triumph in 1932, to complete the destruction of German democracy. In that period, his following grew from the thousands to the tens of millions. Trump's assault on American democracy arguably began in 2020, when he refused to accept his defeat at the polls. His rolling coup attempt has continued and grown since, and along with it the determination of millions of his followers to see him returned to power by whatever means necessary.

In January 2021, fully 71 percent of Republicans polled believed that Joe Biden was not "legitimate." Little wonder that, at Trump's command, thousands of his supporters tried to do something about it on January 6, 2020. The banal normality of the great majority of Trump's supporters, including those who went to the Capitol on January 6, has befuddled many observers. Although private militia groups and white supremacists played a part in the attack, 90 percent of those arrested or charged had no ties to such groups. The majority were middle-class and middle-aged; 40 percent were business owners or white-collar workers. As one fifty-six-year-old Michigan woman explained: "We weren't there to steal things.

We weren't there to do damage. We were just there to overthrow the government."[9]

This is the Republican Party. Trump and his supporters have taken over the party and now seek to take over the country by any means necessary and put an end to the experiment in American liberalism.

How did an antiliberal movement take full control of a major political party for the first time since the antebellum South controlled the Democratic Party? The Republican Party leadership played a critical role—or, rather, refused to play one. It has always been the task of party leaders to control the more disruptive elements of their coalition. Throughout the past century, both political parties have at one time or another had to suppress the more extreme antiliberal forces that were part of their coalition—Roosevelt with the followers of Huey Long, for instance; Harry Truman with the Dixiecrats; Eisenhower/Nixon with McCarthy; Goldwater with the Birchers; George W. Bush with the Islamophobic, anti-immigrant right. They have done so hesitantly, tardily in many cases, and always in the hope of holding on to extremist voters while distancing themselves from their extremist leaders. As a result, these movements until 2016 had to find their outlets outside the two parties, in various third-party candidacies like those of Wallace and Buchanan, or in movements nominally outside the political system but with significant influence inside, like the Klan, the Birchers, and the Tea Party.

The Republican Party leadership did an increasingly poor job of controlling its more extreme elements, especially while in opposition. First during the Clinton presidency and then during the Obama presidency, the Republican conservative "establishment" ceded party leadership more and more to antiliberal forces. When these antiliberals were given free rein to shape the nature of the attack on the Democrats, their strength within the party grew. Instead of fighting back, establishment Republican leaders either got out of the way or joined the antiliberal assault. This lack of courage and commitment to defend liberal-conservative principles, however, also reflected new political and demographic realities. After resisting Trump at first, before the size of his following within the party became clear, establishment party leaders were happy to ride Trump's coattails if it meant getting paid off with hundreds of conservative court appointments, including three Supreme Court justices, tax cuts, immigration restrictions, and deep reductions in regulations on business.

Yet Trump's triumph was also a hostile takeover. The movement's passion was and is for Trump, not the party. GOP primary voters chose Trump over the various flavors of establishment Republicanism (Jeb Bush, Marco

Rubio). After Trump's election, his voters continued to regard establishment Republicans as enemies. Longtime party heroes like Paul Ryan were cast into oblivion for disparaging Trump. Even staunch supporters such as Jeff Sessions eventually became villains, when they would not do as Trump demanded. Those who survived had a difficult balancing act: to use Trump's appeal to pass the Republican agenda while also controlling Trump's excesses, which they worried could ultimately threaten the party's interests.

The takeover extended beyond the leadership. Modern political parties are an ecosystem of interest groups, lobby organizations, job-seekers, campaign donors, and intellectuals. All have a stake in the party's viability; all ultimately depend for their own viability on being roughly aligned with the party's positions; and so all had to make their peace with Trump, too. Conservative publications that once opposed him as unfit for the presidency, like the *National Review* under editor Rich Lowry, had to reverse course or lose readership and funding. Pundits had to adjust to their pro-Trump audiences—and were rewarded handsomely when they did. Donors who had opposed Trump during the primaries fell into line, if only to preserve some influence on the issues that mattered to them. Advocacy organizations that had previously worked to hold the Republican

Party to certain principles either became advocates for Trump or lost clout.

It was no surprise that elected officials increasingly feared taking on the Trump movement, and that Republican job-seekers kept silent or made show-trial-like apologies for past criticism of Trump. Ambition is a powerful antidote to moral qualms. But it wasn't just ambition. There has also been something distinctly tribal in establishment Republicans' refusal to cross Trump and the party leadership, even temporarily, when that party leadership turned in an antiliberal direction. Especially revealing was the behavior of Republican elder statesmen, former secretaries of state in their eighties or nineties like George Shultz, James Baker, and Henry Kissinger, who had no further ambitions for high office and seemingly nothing to lose by speaking out. Despite their known abhorrence of everything Trump stood for, these old lions refused to criticize him publicly. Little wonder that the younger Republican establishment stars still hoping for a future in the party have also kept silent, lest they alienate important Republican policy constituencies. Whatever they thought about Trump, Republican elders disliked Hillary Clinton, Barack Obama, and the Democrats more. Again, this is not so unusual. German conservatives accommodated Adolf Hitler partly because they hated and feared the socialists more than they opposed the Nazis, with whom, after all, they shared many basic prejudices.

The acquiescence of almost the entire Republican Party to the leadership of Trump and his antiliberal followers was, of course, a critical factor in the movement's triumph. It is hard to measure the percentage of voters committed heart and soul to Trump, as opposed to voters who found Trump disagreeable but who voted for him anyway because he was the Republican nominee against the reviled Hillary Clinton of 2016 or the reviled Joe Biden today. According to a poll taken in January 2023, almost 30 percent of Republican voters said they would follow Trump out of the Republican Party if he decided to run as an independent. But what about the rest of the party? Romney won the same share of Republican voters in 2012 (93 percent) that Trump won in 2016 (92 percent). Did Republican voters not care about the difference between these very different candidates? Or had the whole body of Republicans shifted in an antiliberal direction as the party's antiliberal faction grew and its leaders, including even Romney himself in 2012, increasingly played to it?

The latter explanation seems the most likely. Those who had previously supported liberal conservatives may have been troubled by Trump's behavior and his flouting of the norms. But many of them took the same pleasure in Trump's attack on the liberal "elites" as their fellow antiliberal Republicans. Nor were they entirely immune to Trump's appeal to racism and anti-immigrant sentiments, as Romney showed in his 2012 campaign.

The broad liberal consensus that increasingly dominated both parties in the decades following World War Two was driven not by the unstoppable force of liberalism but by events and struggles—the Depression, World War Two, and the Cold War—and by the growing political involvement and influence of ethnic minorities, women, and Black people, all of whom put pressure on both parties to live up to the nation's liberal principles. Mid-twentieth-century America produced a new birth of freedom along multiple fronts, driven by a powerful coalition of groups seeking equal rights for themselves and providing the political energy and support for liberal reforms for others.

Such fervor does not last forever, however, as Jefferson lamented during the Revolution, and as Lincoln observed in his Lyceum Speech in 1838. When a people finally acquire the rights that were denied them, they tend to move on to life's other problems. When they are less concerned about their own rights, they become less concerned about rights in general. This happened to Americans after the perilous early years of the Revolution and the young republic. The American system was founded at a time of high anxiousness about rights, but thereafter only those whose rights had not been recognized cared about perfecting the American regime as Lincoln hoped. Everyone else, except handfuls of committed liberal ideologues like the abolitionists, tended to indifference except when confronted by crises that touched them personally.

Many immigrants in the United States have gone through a similar evolution. By demanding that the nation live up to its liberal principles, immigrant groups fought to eliminate the legal and informal barriers to their full inclusion as equals in American society. They have demanded that their rights be respected both by government and in communities, in both public and private behavior. They have demanded to be treated as first-class American citizens, equal in every respect to the white Protestant immigrants who arrived in the New World before them. That was why many immigrants joined the Democratic Party in the 1920s and '30s—not because of government economic programs, although those were welcome, but because the immigrants were themselves welcome in the party and could make their voices heard through it.

Once they attain these goals, however, their fervor for liberalism has often faded. "I've got mine" is among the most basic of human sentiments. By the 1950s, many Americans of Irish Catholic and German ancestry, once treated as immigrant pariahs, had joined white antiliberals in denouncing all things foreign and non-white as "communist." The McCarthy movement, whatever else it may have been, represented a new alliance of conservative Catholics and white supremacists, something that had been unthinkable in the Klan-dominated 1920s. Americans of German ancestry, eager to put questions about their loyalty during the wars behind them, also took part in white attacks on various "others."

The historic movement of white ethnic voters from the Democratic to the Republican Party, which began in the late 1960s and peaked with the emergence of the "Reagan Democrats" in the 1980s, may have had many causes, including upward economic mobility. But among the most important factors was that these once-oppressed groups no longer felt oppressed and therefore did not feel they needed the further protection of liberalism. They had, for all intents and purposes, joined white America. With the help of the Declaration's principles, the Bill of Rights, and the amended Constitution, and—an important factor—their equal right and opportunity to vote, they had forced their way into substantial political, economic, and even social equality with the very people who had once tried to keep them down. It was not their problem anymore. In fact, having forced their own admittance into the white American club, they were no longer averse to the exclusion of others—and especially the waves of non-white immigrants that began to flood into the country following the Immigration Act of 1965.

It is no secret that among the leading factors that gave rise first to the Tea Party and then to the Trump movement has been the rise of both legal and illegal immigration over the past almost six decades, but it is also no secret that much of the anti-immigrant sentiment has come from groups that were themselves once immigrants. This is certainly true of the white European ethnic groups that came to the United States in the second half of the nineteenth and first half of the twentieth century. But recent polls and elections have shown that some of the more recent arrivals, including American citizens of Latin background, are just as opposed to Latin immigration as white Protestants, especially illegal immigration. With their relative freedom secure, many are also free to act on their own conservative religious inclinations.

This is not to say that these immigrant groups, both old and new, would lead the charge against immigration. But they were more tolerant of or even sympathetic to such impulses in a Republican Party that was otherwise serving their needs as they saw them. The Obama presidency aroused latent racism in many voters, including even those who voted for Obama in 2012 but then voted for Trump in 2016. Although some analysts, as usual, want to explain this phenomenon as a response to economic insecurity or other economic reasons, close analysis has shown that white working-class voters who switched from Obama to Trump did so primarily for reasons of race, not class.[10] The main thing that happened to those voters between 2012 and 2016 was not economic regression and rising inequality. It was Obama, and then it was Trump.

All this has left few dissenting voices within the Republican ecosystem. The Republican Party today is a zombie party. Its leaders go through the motions of governing in pursuit of traditional Republican goals, wrestling over infrastructure spending and foreign policy, even as real power in the party is wielded by Trump and his antiliberal movement. From the uneasy and sometimes contentious partnership during Trump's four years in office, the party has become an active enabler of Trump's efforts to complete the coup d'état he launched after the 2020 election. And even though there are still "establishment" Republicans in the party, like McConnell and Romney, who can see perfectly clearly where the party is taking the country—as Romney says, "A very large portion of my party doesn't believe in the Constitution"—they have been unwilling to risk their political careers by resisting.[11]

With the party firmly under his thumb, Trump is now waging his rebellion against the Constitution on separate fronts. One is normal, legitimate political competition, whereby Trump runs for office and Republicans criticize Biden's policies, feed and fight the culture wars, and in general behave like a typical hostile opposition. The other front is outside the bounds of constitutional and democratic competition and in the realm of illegal or extralegal efforts to undermine the electoral process. The two are intimately related, because the Republican Party has used its institutional power in the political sphere to shield Trump and his followers from the consequences of their illegal and extralegal activities in the lead-up to January 6. Party leaders have run interference for the Trump movement in the sphere of legitimate politics, using the power of Congress to undermine faith in the justice system and American government more generally, while cheering on the January 6 perpetrators, turning them into martyrs and heroes, and thereby greatly encouraging illegal acts in the future.

Trump may lack what Vermeule calls "a substantive comprehensive theory of the good," but he is the one who commands the allegiance of his millions and millions of supporters.[12] If it is his "narcissistic" desire to reclaim the White House, his followers have shown that they are prepared to do whatever it may take to help him achieve that goal, and neither the Republican Party leadership nor the 50 percent of the party not entirely in the thrall of Trump shows any inclination to prevent it.

The political trends over the past few years are, in fact, strikingly similar to those that preceded the Civil War. Then, too, the two parties spent the decade before the war sorting themselves into two hostile and relatively monolithic blocs. The two national parties of the mid-nineteenth century, the Whigs and the Democrats, fractured along liberal and antiliberal lines, which coincided with the North-South boundary. The Democrats, who once had at least a competitive Northern wing, became entirely the party of the South. The Whig Party collapsed and was replaced by a Republican Party that was an amalgam of Northern Whigs, Northern Democrats, and a collection of Northern antislavery and Free Soil parties. In the 1860 election, Lincoln carried every Northern state. The Democratic Party split and ran a Northern candidate, Stephen Douglass, who won only one state (Missouri), and a Southern Democratic candidate, John C. Breckenridge, who took every Southern state (plus Maryland) except Virginia, Tennessee, and Kentucky, which were won by a third-party candidate. The result of that election was civil war. The South did not even wait for Lincoln to begin governing before it seceded.

Today Democrats and Republicans have similarly sorted themselves to the point where the victory of one has become intolerable to the other. If Trump is the nominee, but does not win the election outright, he is sure to declare the election fraudulent, as he has in both previous elections, including the one he won in 2016 (when he denied that he had lost the popular vote). When he claims fraud, he will have the full support of the Republican Party he controls.

What happens then? The likely answer is not civil war, although some amount of violence is inevitable given the weaponry available to all Americans and the increasing number of politically and racially motivated violent incidents in the country over the past few years. But that doesn't mean the nation is safe. It is just as likely that Trump's supporters will refuse to recognize an election that their leader does not win. They are likely to declare a Biden second term illegitimate and refuse to accept its authority. Several states might even band together in a pro-Trump confederacy, defying the federal government collectively. What would happen then? Would a President Joe Biden send force to bring the states back into the Union, as Lincoln did, and as Andrew Jackson threatened to do in 1830? It seems unlikely. One real prospect in the event Trump loses, therefore, is national dissolution.

And what if Trump wins? Who will stop him from fulfilling his election promise to seek "retribution"? With all the immense power of the American presidency, with his ability to control and direct the Justice Department, the FBI, the IRS, the intelligence services, and the military, what will prevent him from using the power of the state to go after his political enemies? Republicans in Congress? And if Trump himself has no agenda other than power and revenge, what about those who will staff his administration? Can the Constitution and American liberal democracy survive the arrival in power of a whole administration full of antiliberal intellectuals and policy makers? Indeed, one wonders how long will Democrats, who still make up half the country and who control the governorships and statehouses of many of the richest and most populous states, stand by passively while a second Trump administration dismantles the liberal democratic system? Or might they be the ones to declare Trump another Hitler—democratically chosen, yes, but nevertheless a clear and present danger to America's liberal democratic institutions?

Americans today may find such scenarios shocking, but the founding generation would not have, nor would Americans throughout most of the nineteenth century. Threats of nullification and even secession were common in the eight decades following the Revolution. Shays' Rebellion in 1786 was, as Gordon Wood observes, "only the climactic episode in one long insurrection" by the people of western Massachusetts. During the War of 1812, it was New England that threatened to secede.[13] In 1830, it was South Carolina, and of course by 1860, following the election of Lincoln, it was the entire South.

This is the flip side of Americans' Lockean heritage. The United States was founded on the principle that a people may overthrow or sever their allegiance to their government if they believe it is not performing its primary function of protecting their rights. In the still-formative years of the nation, when citizens felt the government was not protecting their interests, it was not surprising that some refused to accept its authority, claiming, rightly or wrongly, that it was not fulfilling this one essential task.

Two centuries later, the idea of nullification or secession may seem more exotic, but the basic facts of the American system remain unchanged. As James Wilson put it during the debates over ratification, the Constitution would acquire "value and authority" only with the people's acceptance.[14] Although the Constitution was meant to be binding once adopted, and the process for amending it was made deliberately arduous, it was true at the founding and it remains true today that without broad popular acceptance of the system's legitimacy the voluntary compact could collapse. At that point, the Union could be held together only by the force of the federal government acting in quasi-tyrannical fashion.

This was one of many reasons why the American founding generation was anxious about whether the government they created could possibly last. Was popular self-government—government "of the people, by the people, and for the people," as Lincoln later put it—really possible? Madison and the founders hoped that they were establishing the new system on a solid foundation of interest. But they understood that there also had to be something more, a love of freedom as an abstract ideal, a willingness to compromise, and above all a willingness to fight not only for one's own rights but for everyone else's rights, too. This was the "republican virtue" they believed necessary to hold the system together. Madison and his colleagues agreed that it was "chimerical" to believe that any form of government could "secure liberty and happiness without any virtue in the people." If there was "no virtue among us," Madison believed, "we are in a wretched situation."[15]

Wretched indeed. In the debates over the Constitution in 1787 and 1788, the anti-Federalists warned that Madison's idea of defending liberalism against the natural vices of human nature by pitting interest against interest, ambition against ambition, would not work. The people, they warned, would not always be virtuous. "Virtue will slumber," Patrick Henry warned. "The wicked will be continually watching: Consequently you will be undone."

The "wicked" have now shown themselves, but do Americans see them for what they are? Americans are so used to partisan political conflict that they may not be able to see what is different this time. This is true even of many Democrats. They think they are still fighting Reagan or Bush. They thought the Republican Party was evil then and don't see why it is different now. In this sense they are just as blinded by partisanship as "establishment" Republicans like McConnell. They wear their *D*'s on their chest, just as Republicans wear their *R*'s, and cannot see that this is not just the usual partisan fight.

What we are witnessing, however, is not a political battle but a rebellion. The events of January 6, 2021, proved that Trump and his most die-hard supporters are prepared to defy constitutional and democratic norms, just as revolutionary movements have in the past. Though it may have been shocking to see normal, decent Americans condoning a violent assault on the Capitol, that event demonstrated that Americans as a people are not as exceptional as their founding principles and institutions. Europeans who joined fascist movements in the 1920s and '30s were also from the middle classes. No doubt many of them were good parents and neighbors, too. People do things as part of a mass movement that they would not do as individuals, especially if they are convinced that others are out to destroy their way of life.

Today Trump supporters see the events of January 6 as a patriotic defense of the nation. Trump has returned to the explosive rhetoric of that day, insisting that he won in a "landslide" in 2020, that the "radical left Democrat communist party" stole the presidency in the "most corrupt, dishonest, and unfair election in the history of our country." He has promised to seek revenge against those who he believes brought him down in 2020. Nor can one assume that the various right-wing militias, the Three Percenters and Oath Keepers, would again play a subordinate role when the next riot unfolds. Veterans who assaulted the Capitol told police officers that they had fought for their country before and were fighting for it again. Trump has consistently declared, "There is no way [the Democrats] win elections without cheating. There's no way." So, if the results come in showing another Democratic victory, Trump's supporters will know what to do. Just as "generations of patriots" gave "their sweat, their blood and even their very lives" to build America, Trump told his supporters on January 6, so today "we have no choice. We have to fight" to restore "our American birthright."

That fight is now once again upon us. The battles that Americans have fought in the past must be fought again and again. Can Americans rise to the occasion again? More specifically, can Republican voters? It really is up to them. Let's stipulate that there is much about modern American liberalism they don't like, that many liberal policies don't work or are ill-advised, that the Democrats on many issues have been too much swayed by a progressive left that is just as opposed to American liberalism as the right. Even if that is true, is it worth overthrowing the entire system, as so many antiliberal conservatives today demand? Is that what the average Republican voters have signed up for? One suspects not, but their indifference to the threat posed by Trump has made the dissolution of American liberal democracy possible. If American democracy explodes in this 2024 election year, it will be because Republican voters let it happen.

The tragic irony is that if Americans can get through this coming crisis with their liberal democracy intact, then the greatest danger may have passed. Trump's movement is not unique, but Trump probably is. His fanatical narcissism, his lack of regard for anyone but himself, his demand for constant adoration, his fury at those who criticize him, and his repeatedly demonstrated willingness to use the power of government for his own personal purposes, including exacting revenge against his enemies, puts him in a special category. Americans are unlikely to find another like him running for office anytime soon.

Meanwhile, the overall long-term prospects for American liberalism are actually bright, if only because the demographic shift is a reality that can't be blinked away. White supremacy is another Lost Cause. As America becomes increasingly multiracial, multiethnic, and multicultural, and as it becomes impossible for any single ethnoreligious group to dominate American politics and society, the appeal of liberalism as the only means of holding such a society together should grow. Many white people may not change their attitudes toward other racial and ethnic groups—after all, they haven't changed in two hundred years—but their ability to fight to preserve their hierarchies will diminish because they will be too badly outnumbered. That is why 2024 is the year when the antiliberals hope to overthrow the system. It may be their last chance. Whether they succeed or not will depend on the American people, Democrats and Republicans alike. Americans who believe in the liberalism of the Revolution and the founding will have to fight for it, again. If they do not, whether out of complacency or indifference, American liberal government, and the freedoms it provides us all, will be no more.

Acknowledgments

I owe thanks to many people who have helped make this book possible. As always, I am indebted to the Brookings Institution for its support over many years and particularly to Stephen and Barbara Friedman and Phil Knight, as well as others who have provided support for the work of Brookings scholars like me. My friend and mentor Roger Hertog has also generously supported my work for many years. I also want to thank friends and colleagues who took the time to read my manuscript and offered many valuable suggestions, especially Michael O'Hanlon and Leon Wieseltier. On this as on so much of my work, I have relied on the knowledge and wisdom and friendship of Gary Schmitt. I cannot thank enough my editor, Andrew Miller, who keeps alive the great tradition of editors at Knopf, always thoughtful, always supportive, always seeking excellence. I am most grateful to my agent Rafe Sagalyn, a man of kindness and sagacity. Suzanne Maloney at Brookings has been an exemplary and incredibly supportive boss and colleague. Thanks also to Sophia Hart, whose support I counted on throughout the writing and production of this book.

I must also express deep thanks to the editing collective known as the Kagan Nuland family. We have gotten to the point where we are all editing one another at one time or another, and, given the distribution of talents, I am the greatest beneficiary of that arrangement. More than ever, I now look to my children, Leni and David, for clarity and insight. I have no greater editor and partner than my wife, Victoria Nuland, who, though occasionally busy with other things, has always taken time to make me a better writer. I stand as always in loving awe of her.

This book is dedicated to the memory of my dear friend Fred Hiatt. When the founders imagined the virtuous citizenry they hoped would populate their new nation, it was of Fred they dreamed.

Notes

Introduction

1. Matthew Dallek, *Birchers: How the John Birch Society Radicalized the American Right* (New York: Basic Books, 2022), 20.
2. Daniel Bell, ed., *The Radical Right*, 3rd ed. (New York: Anchor Books, 1964), 10.
3. Quoted in Alan Brinkley, *Voices of Protest: Huey Long, Father Coughlin, and the Great Depression* (New York: Alfred A. Knopf, 1982), 70. The Dartmouth scholar Jeffrey Hart observed that Wallace offered "freedom from the conventional taboos. The man says what he thinks. Wouldn't it be fun to do that? Even more impressive, he has actually prospered by saying what he thinks, by being abrasive and obnoxious" (quoted in Matthew Continetti, *The Right: The Hundred Year War for American Conservatism* [New York: Basic Books, 2022], 184).
4. Quoted in Continetti, *The Right*, 11.
5. Stephen Kantrowitz, *Ben Tillman & the Reconstruction of White Supremacy* (Chapel Hill: University of North Carolina Press, 2000), 132, 136, 278.
6. On the absurdity of Tillman representing himself as one of the poor farmers fighting the "aristocrats," see ibid., 134. He claimed to be "organiz[ing] the common people against the aristocracy" (135).
7. The idea of American conservatives as "conservers" of liberalism has been well articulated by the Harvard political philosopher Harvey

Mansfield: "I think today that the principal task of conservatism is to save liberalism from the liberals" (quoted in Continetti, *The Right,* 412). Daniel Bell called McCarthy "an Umstürzmensch, a man who wants to tear up society but has no plan of his own . . . a wrecker" (Bell, ed., *Radical Right,* x). As Kevin Phillips put it in the 1970s, there were conservatives "whose game it is to quote English poetry and utter neo-Madisonian benedictions over the interests and institutions of establishment liberalism." And then there were those who had "more in common with Andrew Jackson than with Edmund Burke" and who aimed "to build cultural siege-cannon out of the populist steel of Idaho, Mississippi, and working-class Milwaukee, and then blast the eastern liberal establishment to ideo-institutional smithereens" (quoted in Continetti, *The Right,* 232).

1: The Radicalism of the American Revolution

1. Quoted in Harry V. Jaffa, *Crisis of the House Divided* (Chicago: University of Chicago Press, 2022), 316.

2. Isser Woloch, *Eighteenth-Century Europe: Tradition and Progress, 1715–1789* (New York: W. W. Norton, 1982), 238–40. As Woloch observes, "Neither Voltaire nor the other philosophers can be regarded as democratic, apart from their belief in equality before the law. Their view of the common people was condescending and skeptical even while sympathetic. . . . At best, most *philosophes* visualized a very long-term evolution in which education would eventually filter down to the masses and modify their behavior. . . . They were, if one must label them, liberal elitists without a conscience."

3. Ibid., 258–59.

4. Quoted in Gordon S. Wood, *The Creation of the American Republic, 1776–1787* (Chapel Hill: University of North Carolina Press, 1969, 1998), 30.

5. Ibid., 18.

6. As the British historian Linda Colley has explained, Protestantism had by the eighteenth century become the core of British identity. It was what Britons repeatedly fought and died for, against Spain, France, and other Catholic great powers; it was what they had exe-

cuted a king and invited foreign invasion for. Therefore, "more than anything else, it was this shared religious allegiance combined with recurrent wars that permitted a sense of British national identity to emerge" (Linda Colley, *Britons: Forging the Nation, 1707–1837,* rev. ed. [New Haven, Conn.: Yale University Press, 2009], 6, 18).

7. Gordon S. Wood, *The Radicalism of the American Revolution* (New York: Alfred A. Knopf, 1992), 111.

8. Even among the English Protestants there was no suggestion of equality. "Non-conformist Protestant dissent was granted somewhat broader toleration, but was also excluded from the 'establishment'" (Woloch, *Eighteenth-Century Europe,* 30).

9. This was deliberate; it was "fundamental to the 'mixed government' concept and tradition." Most voting occurred in "corporate" boroughs, where the right to vote for Parliament had been granted by the Crown. The great majority of these "rotten boroughs" had but a few hundred easily manipulated voters and therefore served as sinecures where the king and his ministers could place loyal supporters. According to Woloch, "out of 405 borough deputies, only 112 were ever chosen by more than five hundred voters" (ibid., 33).

10. Max M. Edling, *A Revolution in Favor of Government: Origins of the U.S. Constitution and the Making of the American State* (New York and Oxford, U.K.: Oxford University Press, 2003), 52. That included the tens of thousands of inhabitants of the growing cities of Manchester and Birmingham, which were not represented in Parliament at all.

11. "The vast majority of the British population did not possess any direct access to the state" (Wood, *Creation,* 174–75).

12. Jonathan Israel, *The Expanding Blaze: How the American Revolution Ignited the World, 1775–1848* (Princeton, N.J., and Oxford, U.K.: Princeton University Press, 2017), 5–6.

13. Edling, *Revolution,* 51; Paul Langford, *A Polite and Commercial People: England, 1727–1783* (Oxford, U.K.: Oxford University Press, 1989), 692.

14. Under the first two Hanoverian kings, George I and George II, the government was effectively run by the "prime minister," Robert Walpole, whose control of Parliament on the king's behalf was so great that critics referred to the "Robinocracy." By the middle of the eighteenth century, even some Britons were complaining of the

growing centralization of power and the king's "corrupt" influence in Parliament. When George III inherited the throne in the 1760s and proceeded to oust William Pitt, the Whigs who had dominated British politics since the Glorious Revolution denounced him as a would-be tyrant trying to replicate the French monarchy (Woloch, *Eighteenth-Century Europe*, 30, 34).

15. Quoted in Jack P. Greene, *The Intellectual Construction of America: Exceptionalism and Identity from 1492 to 1800* (Chapel Hill: University of North Carolina Press, 1993), 135.

16. Crèvecoeur: "The idle may be employed, the useless become useful, and the poor become rich" in the sense of possessing "cleared lands, cattle, good houses, good clothes, and an increase of people to enjoy them" (quoted in ibid., 104).

17. Jefferson's ideal of the "yeoman" farmer was just that, an ideal. In his imagining, "yeoman" farmers were independent and farmed only for subsistence, and therefore impervious to the pressures of a city-based economic order, which Jefferson despised. In fact, the great majority of American farmers were full participants in the national and international market.

18. David P. Szatmary, *Shays' Rebellion: The Making of an Agrarian Insurrection* (Amherst: University of Massachusetts Press, 1980), 1.

19. Quoted in Robert Kagan, *Dangerous Nation: America's Foreign Policy from Its Earliest Days to the Dawn of the Twentieth Century* (New York: Alfred A. Knopf, 2007), 16.

20. Frederic L. Paxson, *History of the American Frontier, 1763–1893* (New York: Houghton Mifflin, 1924; reprint, Simon Publications, 2001), 77.

21. Edling, *Revolution*, 56.

22. Quoted in Greene, *Intellectual Construction*, 180.

23. Quoted in ibid., 116.

24. Quoted in Szatmary, *Shays' Rebellion*, 14.

25. Wood, *Radicalism*, 18.

26. "I have groped in dark Obscurity, till of late," Adams complained, "and had but just become known, and gained a small degree of Reputation, when this execrable Project was set on foot for my ruin as well as that of America in general, and of Great Britain" (Kagan, *Dangerous Nation*, 36).

27. Wood, *Creation,* 112. "Whatever the social reality prior to the Revolution may have been—and the evidence indicates that social mobility was considerably lessening—American Whigs sensed a hardening of the social mold, aggravated by the influx of new royal officials since 1763" (ibid., 79).

28. On the fears of tyranny expressed by leading colonists, see ibid., 38–42.

29. Ibid., 178.

30. To add to the colonists' grievances, Parliament passed the Quebec Act, which prohibited them from the land and trade between the Ohio and Mississippi rivers and, at least as infuriating to the Protestant colonists, allowed the Québecois to practice their Catholic religion.

31. Edling, *Revolution,* 104.

32. Quoted in Kagan, *Dangerous Nation,* 32–33.

33. It may be that some Britons since 1688 had come to believe in "natural rights" in some form, or at least some blurriness had developed on the question of whether or not the rights the king was bound to protect existed a priori. The Whig interpretation of the Revolution of 1688 was that there was "an original contract between the crown and the people." When "the executive part endeavors the subversion and total destruction of the government, the original contract is thereby broke" (quoted in Steve Pincus, *1688: The First Modern Revolution* [New Haven, Conn.: Yale University Press, 2009], 15). Everyone in the eighteenth century knew that the English had justified their Glorious Revolution by a violation of the assumed contract by James II. And by 1776, Americans had in a like way come to describe their Revolution as resulting from a similar break in "the original contract between King and people" (Wood, *Creation,* 270).

34. Alexander Hamilton, "The Farmer Refuted," Feb. 23, 1775, Founders Online, National Archives. Did Americans base their rights on ancient "charters and compacts" inherited from England, one colonist asked rhetorically, "or did they deduce them from a higher source, *the laws of God and nature?*" (Wood, *Creation,* 291).

35. Thomas Jefferson, *Notes on the State of Virginia,* 1785.

36. Had the Revolution not occurred, the revolutionary historian David

Ramsay believed, Americans' "frugality, industry, and simplicity of manners, would have been lost in imitation of British extravagance, idleness, and false refinements" (quoted in Wood, *Creation*, 110).

37. Quoted in ibid., 48.

38. Wood, *Creation*, 128; Thomas Jefferson, letter to Thomas Nelson, May 16, 1776, National Archives.

39. This was unlike the French Revolution of 1789, which began as an effort to constrain the king in similar fashion and ended with the taking down of the monarchy, eliminating the privileges of the aristocracy, and attacking the established church.

40. Thomas Paine, "The Forester's Letters," 1776, Bartleby.com.

41. Quoted in Wood, *Creation*, 67.

42. Thomas Jefferson, "A Summary View of the Rights of British America," 1774, *Digital History,* https://www.digitalhistory.uh.edu/disp_textbook.cfm?smtID=3&psid=113.

43. Quoted in Wood, *Creation*, 397.

44. Quoted in ibid., 405.

45. Quoted in ibid., 410.

46. Quoted in ibid., 407.

47. George Washington to John Jay, Aug. 15, 1786, Founders Online, National Archives, https://founders.archives.gov/documents/Washington/04-04-02-0199; *The Federalist,* No. 10, Nov. 22, 1787.

48. Under Napoleon, the Catholic Church, having been all but vanquished by the Revolution, regained its footing with the Concordat of 1801 and would make an even bigger comeback in the period of the Restoration, when the Bourbon monarchy reinstated the Catholic Church as the state religion.

49. Israel, *Expanding Blaze*, 85.

50. Jefferson, *Notes on the State of Virginia.*

51. This, it should be emphasized, was not the traditional Protestant view of the relationship of church and state. Calvin's Geneva was a theocracy, as was the Puritan commonwealth in Massachusetts. Nor was Jefferson's "deism" Protestant, since Protestants believed in Christ the Savior and in the Trinity, whereas Jefferson and other deists thought that was all nonsense. To Jefferson and other Enlightenment thinkers, that central feature of the Christian faith was pure

superstition—"once we made God in our image," Voltaire insisted, "the divine cult was perverted" (Voltaire, "On Superstition," 1767).

52. Some scholars who believe in the "originalist" interpretation of the Constitution misunderstand Jefferson's later comment, when asked about interpreting the Constitution, that people should return "to the time when the Constitution was adopted" and "recollect the spirit manifest in the debates" rather than trying to find "what meaning may be squeezed out of the text, or invented against it." The "spirit" he was referring to was the extreme concern for securing natural rights, which he had predicted would quickly fade once the immediate crisis was over, a prediction in which he no doubt felt vindicated almost four decades later.

53. Paxson, *History of the American Frontier*, 6.

54. Quoted in Greene, *Intellectual Construction*, 174. Congress passed legislation in 1790 clarifying that immigration was open to free white people—i.e., not to free Black people or, later, immigrants from China and Japan. The Pennsylvania state constitution required only that people be of a certain age, were resident for one year, and paid taxes (ibid., 114). In New York, Gouverneur Morris observed, it was a "matter of indifference" whether someone was born in America (Wood, *Creation*, 169; Ron Chernow, *Alexander Hamilton* [New York: Penguin Books, 2004], 50).

55. Quoted in Sean Wilentz, *The Rise of American Democracy: Jefferson to Lincoln* (New York: W. W. Norton, 2005), 9.

56. "All this changed with the American Revolution. By freeing the colonies from British rule, the Revolution set the stage for formidable attacks on slavery and in turn necessitated a strong defense of slavery" (Paul Finkelman, *Defending Slavery: Proslavery Thought in the Old South* [Boston and New York: Bedford/Macmillan], 16).

57. Locke himself neither endorsed nor criticized slavery. For most Britons, however, as Paul Finkelman notes, "slavery fit perfectly well into a society built on hierarchy" (ibid., 20). In the modern era, Spain, France, and other Catholic countries had engaged in the slave trade, but the Protestant British, with their superior navy, had all but monopolized it over the course of the seventeenth and eighteenth centuries.

58. Quoted in ibid., 16–17.

59. Ibid., 17.

60. Wood, *Creation*, 83.

61. Quoted in Greene, *Intellectual Construction*, 154.

62. Chernow, *Hamilton*, 307. Samuel Johnson also observed, "We hear the loudest yelps for liberty among the drivers of negroes" (quoted in Finkelman, *Defending Slavery*, 20).

63. Jefferson, *Notes on the State of Virginia*.

64. Ibid.

65. Quoted in Finkelman, *Defending Slavery*, 57.

66. Ibid., 19.

67. The Southern delegates also made clear that, without representation for slavery, there would be an end to the Union. Governor William R. Davie warned that his state, North Carolina, would "never confederate" unless slaves were counted for representation, and that if slaves were not counted for apportionment, "the business [of the convention] was at an end" (quoted in ibid., 25). In the debate over the slave trade, South Carolina's Governor John Rutledge told the convention that the "true question at present is whether the southern states shall or shall not be parties to the union." Pinckney declared that a prohibition of the slave trade would be "an exclusion of S. Carolina from the union," because "S. Carolina and Georgia cannot do without slaves" (quoted in ibid.).

68. By calculating each state's electoral votes according to the sum of their two senators and the size of their delegation in the House, which, thanks to the three-fifths clause, inflated the slaveholding states' representation, the Constitution guaranteed, seemingly in perpetuity, that the slave states would wield more power than their voting populations alone would have justified.

69. Quoted in Finkelman, *Defending Slavery*, 26.

70. Quoted in Wood, *Creation*, 500.

Notes

2: The Antiliberal Tradition in America

1. Quoted in Gordon S. Wood, *The Creation of the American Republic, 1776–1787* (Chapel Hill: University of North Carolina Press, 1969, 1998), 426.
2. W. J. Cash, *The Mind of the South* (New York: Vintage Books, 1991), 61.
3. Quoted in Robert Kagan, *Dangerous Nation: America's Foreign Policy from Its Earliest Days to the Dawn of the Twentieth Century* (New York: Alfred A. Knopf, 2007), 231.
4. Ibid., 190.
5. Quoted in ibid., 231.
6. Quoted in ibid., 196.
7. Quoted in ibid., 194–95.
8. Quoted in Robert P. Forbes, "The Missouri Controversy and Sectionalism," in *Congress and the Emergence of Sectionalism: From the Missouri Compromise to the Age of Jackson,* ed. Paul Finkelman and Donald R. Kennon (Athens: University of Ohio Press, 2008), 82–83.
9. Quoted in Kagan, *Dangerous Nation,* 199.
10. Quoted in ibid., 198.
11. William Plumer Jr., Letters to William Plumer, March 4, 1820, William Plumer Papers, Library of Congress.
12. Quoted in Kagan, *Dangerous Nation,* 197.
13. Quoted in Paul Finkelman, *Defending Slavery: Proslavery Thought in the Old South* (Boston and New York: Bedford/Macmillan), 39.
14. Cash, *Mind of the South,* 66–67.
15. Ibid., 90.
16. As Cash explained, "Let a Yankee abolitionist be caught spreading his propaganda in the land, let a southerner speak out boldly his conviction that the north was essentially right about the institution, and he was not merely frowned on, cursed, hated; he was, in this country long inured to violence, dealt with more pointedly and personally: he was hanged or tarred or horsewhipped" (ibid., 89).
17. George Fitzhugh, *Sociology for the South; or, The Failure of Free Society* (London: Forgotten Books, 2015; originally published 1854), 206.
18. Fitzhugh, quoted in Finkelman, *Defending Slavery,* 195.

19. Quoted in Katherine Stewart, *The Power Worshippers: Inside the Dangerous Rise of Religious Nationalism* (New York: Bloomsbury, 2019), 110.

20. Quoted in Kagan, *Dangerous Nation*, 199.

21. Quoted in ibid., 203.

22. Quoted in ibid., 204.

23. William W. Freehling, *The Road to Disunion: Secessionists at Bay, 1776–1854* (New York and Oxford, U.K.: Oxford University Press, 1990), viii.

24. Quoted in "Lovejoy's Influence on John Brown," *Magazine of History*, Sept.–Oct. 1916, 98.

25. Abraham Lincoln, "The Perpetuation of Our Political Institutions," address before the Young Men's Lyceum of Springfield, Ill., Jan. 27, 1838. "I do not mean to say, that the scenes of the revolution *are now* or *ever will* be entirely forgotten; but that like everything else, they must fade upon the memory of the world, and grow more and more dim by the lapse of time. In history, we hope, they will be read of, and recounted, so long as the bible shall be read;—but even granting that they will, their influence *cannot be* what it heretofore has been. Even then, they *cannot be* so universally known, nor so vividly felt, as they were by the generation just gone to rest. At the close of that struggle, nearly every adult male had been a participator in some of its scenes. The consequence was, that of those scenes, in the form of a husband, a father, a son or brother, a *living history* was to be found in every family—a history bearing the indubitable testimonies of its own authenticity, in the limbs mangled, in the scars of wounds received, in the midst of the very scenes related—a history, too, that could be read and understood alike by all, the wise and the ignorant, the learned and the unlearned.—But *those* histories are gone. They *can* be read no more forever. They *were* a fortress of strength; but, what invading foeman could *never do*, the silent artillery of time *has done;* the leveling of its walls. They are gone.—They *were* a forest of giant oaks; but the all-resistless hurricane has swept over them, and left only, here and there, a lonely trunk, despoiled of its verdure, shorn of its foliage; unshading and unshaded, to murmur in a few

gentle breezes, and to combat with its mutilated limbs, a few more ruder storms, then to sink, and be no more."

26. Quoted in Kagan, *Dangerous Nation,* 202.

27. Quoted in ibid., 228.

28. Quoted in ibid., 229.

29. Quoted in ibid., 261–62.

30. Quoted in ibid., 198.

3: The Triumph of Antiliberalism

1. After some debate, the Electoral College was kept in place, despite the fact that it had been designed in part to protect slavery.

2. Benjamin Butler, speech, in the House of Representatives, 1866.

3. W. J. Cash, *The Mind of the South* (New York: Vintage Books, 1991), 103–4.

4. Ibid., 117.

5. Ibid., 109.

6. Ibid., 107, 116.

7. Even after defeat in the Civil War, the South made clear that the reestablishment of white supremacy in the South, and the removal of all Black political influence, was the sine qua non of their political participation. As one Mississippi leader put it—in 1902, almost four decades after the war—the South would rather have no representation at all in Congress than "return again to the state of affairs existing in the reconstruction period," when African Americans exercised their right to vote (*Congressional Record,* House, 57th Cong., 1st sess. [31 March 1902], 3484, 3486).

8. As Cash notes, the Democratic Party became "the institutionalized incarnation of the will to White Supremacy." It had long since ceased to be "a party *in* the South and became the party *of* the South, a kind of confraternity having in its keeping the whole corpus of southern loyalties, and so irresistibly commanding the allegiance of faithful whites that to doubt it, to question it in any detail, was *ipso facto* to stand branded as a renegade to race, to country, to God" (Cash, *Mind of the South,* 128).

9. Quoted in Stephen Kantrowitz, *Ben Tillman & the Reconstruction of White Supremacy* (Chapel Hill: University of North Carolina Press, 2000), 7.

10. Quoted in ibid., 242.

11. Jonathan Israel, *The Expanding Blaze: How the American Revolution Ignited the World, 1775–1848* (Princeton, N.J., and Oxford, U.K.: Princeton University Press, 2017), 87; Gordon S. Wood, *The Creation of the American Republic, 1776–1787* (Chapel Hill: University of North Carolina Press, 1969, 1998), 428; Israel, *Expanding Blaze,* 88.

12. See John Higham, *Strangers in the Land: Patterns of American Nativism, 1860–1925* (New Brunswick, N.J., and London: Rutgers University Press, 1955, 1983), 6.

13. Richard Brookhiser, *Gentleman Revolutionary: Gouverneur Morris, the Rake Who Wrote the Constitution* (New York: Free Press, 2003), 33.

14. Quoted in John T. McGreevy, *Catholicism and American Freedom: A History* (New York: W. W. Norton, 2003), 54.

15. Ibid., 49, 52–54.

16. Ibid., 23.

17. Quoted in ibid., 75.

18. Roger Daniels, *Coming to America: A History of Immigration and Ethnicity in American Life* (New York: HarperPerennial, 1991), 3.

19. Ibid., 139.

20. Ibid., 124–25.

21. Ibid., 127.

22. Ibid., 130.

23. Ibid., 267–68.

24. Anti-immigration activists warned of "the outcast and offal of society, the vagrant and convict—transported in myriads to our shores, reeking with the accumulated crimes of the whole civilized world" (quoted in ibid., 269).

25. In 1790, Congress passed a law declaring that citizenship was available only to free white persons; this nod to the reality of slavery would, however, be used to prohibit Asian immigrants in the next century.

26. Quoted in Higham, *Strangers in the Land,* 21.

27. Elting E. Morison ed., *The Letters of Theodore Roosevelt*, vol. 7 (Cambridge, Mass.: Harvard University Press, 1954), 824.

28. Not all progressives pushed efforts to make the immigrant assimilate to Anglo-Protestant American norms. Lillian Wald, for example, defined the task as one of "fusing these people who come to us from the old world civilization into . . . a real brotherhood among men"—expressing a sentiment Jefferson and the founders would have understood (quoted in Higham, *Strangers in the Land*, 238).

29. Ibid., 271.

30. The rising radicalism of new labor movements, like the Industrial Workers of the World, was also associated with the many immigrants who took part, even though the leaders of the labor movement in America, like "Big Bill" Haywood and Eugene V. Debs, were American-born and -bred.

31. Higham, *Strangers in the Land*, 154.

32. Madison Grant, *The Passing of the Great Race; Or, the Racial Basis of European History* (New York: Charles Scribner's Sons, 1916), 46.

33. Jonathan P. Spiro, *Defending the Master Race: Conservation, Eugenics, and the Legacy of Madison Grant* (University of Vermont Press, 2009), 373–74.

34. Ibid.

35. Higham, *Strangers in the Land*, 273. Ellsworth Huntington, a Yale professor of geography, president of the American Eugenics Society in the 1930s, and father of the famous scholar Samuel P. Huntington, published *The Character of the Races as Influenced by Physical Environment, Natural Selection and Historical Development* in 1924, in which he warned that if the "tenth of the population having the soundest combination of physical health, good intellect, strong wills, and fine temperaments" was not encouraged to have large families, then the lower tenth, which was having large families, would come to dominate, and the "highest racial values" would be "irrevocably swamped by those of lower caliber."

36. Higham, *Strangers in the Land*, 276, 271.

37. Oscar Handlin and Mary F. Handlin, "The Acquisition of Political Rights by the Jews in the United States," in *American Jewish Year*

Book 1955, ed. Morris Fine (New York: American Jewish Committee, 1955), 60, 67.

38. As Higham argues, "The war virtually swept from the American consciousness the old belief in unrestricted immigration. It did so, very simply, by creating an urgent demand for national unity and homogeneity that practically destroyed . . . the historic confidence in the capacity of American Society to assimilate all men automatically. And with the passing of faith in the melting pot there perished the ideal of American nationality as an unfinished, steadily improving, cosmopolitan blend" (Higham, *Strangers in the Land,* 301).

39. Quoted in Robert Kagan, *The Ghost at the Feast: America and the Collapse of World Order, 1900–1941* (New York: Alfred A. Knopf, 2023), 352.

40. Quoted in Higham, *Strangers in the Land,* 286.

41. Ibid., 288.

42. Quoted in Linda Gordon, *The Second Coming of the KKK: The Ku Klux Klan of the 1920s and the American Political Tradition* (New York: Liveright, 2017), 43.

43. Ibid., 2–3. Alabama's Senator Tom Heflin sang its praises: "God has raised up this great patriotic organization to unmask popery" (quoted in David Burner, *The Politics of Provincialism: The Democratic Party in Transition, 1918–1932* [New York: Alfred A. Knopf, 1968], 87).

44. Gordon, *Second Coming of the KKK,* 2–3, 21.

45. Seymour Martin Lipset, "The Sources of the 'Radical Right,'" in Daniel Bell, ed., *The Radical Right,* 3rd ed. (New York: Anchor Books, 1964), 314.

46. Quoted in Gordon, *Second Coming of the KKK,* 44.

47. Ibid., 164.

48. Ibid.

49. In his last veto statement, Wilson made what turned out to be a final plea for the founders' original liberal vision. He opposed efforts to close "the gates of asylum which have always been open to those who could find nowhere else the right and opportunity of constitutional agitation for what they conceived to be the natural and inalienable rights of men" (Higham, *Strangers in the Land,* 191–93).

50. Quoted in ibid., 300. Even "Silent Cal" uttered enough words to

indicate that he shared the concern of his fellow white Protestants that the Nordic race would deteriorate if mixed too much with other races (ibid., 318).

51. Quoted in ibid., 324.

4: The Civil Rights Revolution

1. The shift became especially noticeable in the midterm elections of 1922, when some of the big Eastern cities that had been predominantly Republican since the late 1890s shifted to the Democrats. In what had been a largely Republican New York City, for instance, the influx of immigrants swelled Democratic ranks (David Burner, *The Politics of Provincialism: The Democratic Party in Transition, 1918–1932* [New York: Alfred A. Knopf, 1968], 105–6).

2. Quoted in ibid., 160–61.

3. Ibid., 203. The Iowa-born evangelical minister Billy Sunday, whose hundreds of revival meetings were attended by tens of millions over two decades, declared himself the "ambassador of God" out "to defy the forces of hell—Al Smith and the rest of them" (quoted in ibid., 202).

4. Walter Lippmann, *Men of Destiny* (Abingdon, U.K., and New York: Routledge, 2003), 8–9. Norris quoted in Burner, *Politics of Provincialism,* 221.

5. In Boston, the Democratic vote rose from 35.5 to 66.8 percent, in Chicago from 20.3 to 46.5 percent, in Pittsburgh from 8.7 to 42.4 percent, in Philadelphia from 12.1 to 39.5 percent. The same was true in the cities of the upper Midwest and Far West: the Democratic vote in Milwaukee went from 9.7 to 53.7 percent, in Cleveland from 9.1 to 45.6 percent, in Minneapolis from 6.3 to 38.8 percent, in Detroit from 7.1 to 36.8 percent, in San Francisco from 6.4 to 49.4 percent, and in Seattle from 6.6 to 31.9 percent ("1928 Presidential Election," Wikipedia, https://en.wikipedia.org).

6. Quoted in John T. McGreevy, *Catholicism and American Freedom: A History* (New York: W. W. Norton, 2003), 148.

7. Quoted in ibid., 150.

8. James T. Patterson, *Grand Expectations: The United States, 1945–1974* (New York and Oxford, U.K.: Oxford University Press, 1996), 20, 23.

9. Quoted in ibid., 21.

10. Since a Republican could never win in the South prior to Hoover's inroads in 1928, the general elections, in which Black people theoretically could vote, were irrelevant.

11. Jonathan Eig, *King: A Life* (New York: Farrar, Straus and Giroux, 2023), 18.

12. Quoted in Harvard Sitkoff, *The Struggle for Black Equality, 1954–1980* (New York: Hill and Wang, 1981), 24.

13. Hubert Humphrey, speech at the Democratic National Convention, July 14, 1948, *American Rhetoric,* https://www.americanrhetoric.com/speeches/huberthumphey1948dnc.html.

14. The Warren Court, which overturned *Plessy,* had been appointed by Roosevelt (five justices), Truman (three justices), and, finally, in the case of Warren, by Eisenhower. The federal district court judge who ordered the state of Arkansas to allow desegregation to go forward was from North Dakota.

15. Sitkoff, *Struggle for Black Equality,* 23–27.

16. Quoted in Eig, *King,* 315.

17. Sitkoff, *Struggle for Black Equality,* 28.

18. Quoted in ibid., 179–80.

5: The Birth of the "New" Right

1. Quoted in Matthew Continetti, *The Right: The Hundred Year War for American Conservatism* (New York: Basic Books, 2022), 128-94, 129–30. Major contributors like Kirk, Richard Weaver, and James J. Kilpatrick celebrated the South's distinctive culture precisely for its defiance of liberalism and its organic traditionalism—the "last nonmaterialist civilization in the western world." "The attack on the southern school system," Weaver wrote, was "but one front of a general attack on the principle of an independent, self-directing order, with a set of values proper to itself."

2. William F. Buckley Jr., *Up from Liberalism* (New York: Arlington House, 1968), 87.

3. Ibid., 29.

4. Daniel Bell, ed., *The Radical Right,* 3rd ed. (New York: Anchor Books, 1962), 21.

5. Ibid., 23.

6. James Madison, *Property, The Papers of James Madison.*

7. Even those critical of Reagan's stance on civil rights complained that he was not continuing to push for progress; more than that, he was actively "turning back the clock." See, for instance, Drew S. Days III, "Turning Back the Clock: The Reagan Administration and Civil Rights," *Harvard Civil Rights–Civil Liberties Law Review* 19 (1984): 309–48.

8. Gary Gerstle, *American Crucible: Race and Nation in the Twentieth Century* (Princeton, N.J., and Oxford, U.K.: Princeton University Press, 2001), 361.

9. Continetti, *The Right,* 289, 291, 300.

10. Christopher Caldwell, "The Southern Captivity of the GOP," *Atlantic,* June 1998, https://www.theatlantic.com.

11. Quoted in Continetti, *The Right,* 330.

12. Gerstle, *American Crucible,* 382.

13. Muzaffar Chishti, Faye Hipsman, and Isabel Ball, "Fifty Years On, the 1965 Immigration and Nationality Act Continues to Reshape the United States," *Migration Information Source,* Oct. 15, 2015, https://www.migrationpolicy.org.

14. Ibid.

15. Samuel P. Huntington, *Who Are We?: The Challenges to America's National Identity* (New York: Simon & Schuster, 2004), xv–xvi.

16. Quoted in Gerstle, *American Crucible,* 381; Continetti, *The Right,* 341.

17. Quoted in Peter Baker and Susan Glasser, *The Divider: Trump in the White House, 2017–2021* (New York: Doubleday, 2022), 15.

18. Continetti, *The Right,* 353. At the end of the Bush years, the anti-liberal conservative Angelo Codevilla charged that the Republican Party, like the Democratic Party, was part of the "Ruling Class" and had "zero claim" to the trust of what he called "the Country Class" (ibid., 355).

19. The "big problem" with having a Southern base was that "southern interests" diverged from "those of the rest of the country." Caldwell

believed the increasingly Southern-dominated Republican Party was passing a "tipping point" at which it would become too conservative for the American public (Caldwell, "Southern Captivity of the GOP").

20. Continetti, *The Right*, 344.

21. Barack Obama, *A Promised Land* (New York: Crown, 2020).

22. Dana Milbank, *The Destructionists: The Twenty-Five-Year Crack-Up of the Republican Party* (New York: Doubleday, 2022), 138.

23. Ibid., 136.

24. Quoted in Liz Halloran, "Gang of 8 Champion Plan, Declare 'Year of Immigration Reform,'" NPR, April 18, 2013, https://www.npr.org.

25. Continetti, *The Right*, 358.

26. "Attitudes on Same-Sex Marriage," Pew Research Center, May 14, 2019, https://www.pewresearch.org.

27. Quoted in Andrew L. Whitehead and Samuel L. Perry, *Taking America Back for God: Christian Nationalism in the United States* (New York and Oxford, U.K.: Oxford University Press, 2020), 131.

28. "45% of Americans Say U.S. Should Be a 'Christian Nation,'" Pew Research Center, Oct. 27, 2022, https://www.pewresearch.org.

29. Whitehead and Perry, *Taking America Back for God*, 56–57.

30. Quoted in Katherine Stewart, *The Power Worshippers: Inside the Dangerous Rise of Religious Nationalism* (New York: Bloomsbury, 2019), 105.

31. Dabney quoted in ibid., 110–11.

32. Although Rushdoony's most sensational prescriptions often get the most attention—for instance, the requirement to stone homosexuals to death—his broader message, that people must choose between the law of God derived from scripture and the law of man derived from reason, that there can be no "neutral" position of accommodation between the two, has become an increasingly significant part of modern antiliberal conservatism. (Dabney quoted in ibid., 113; Rousas John Rushdoony, *The Institutes of Biblical Law*, 100; Whitehead and Perry, *Taking America Back for God*, 11.)

33. When Hawley says in speeches that "there is not one square inch of all creation over which Jesus Christ is not Lord," he is quoting Kuyper and articulating "Dominionist" theology. When the Protes-

tant pastor and father of the Texas senator Ted Cruz, Rafael Cruz, says that "separation of church and state is not in the Constitution" and that the First Amendment was designed to "keep the government out of religion but not to keep religion out of government," he is drawing on Rushdoony and "Dominionism." Even Hawley's latest focus on "manhood" can be traced to Rushdoony, who, like Dabney before him, warned that the public education system in America, by denying the God-decreed subordination of the woman to the man in the family and by letting the state rather than the father provide his children's education, was diminishing "man's calling to exercise dominion" and left men "emasculated" (Rushdoony, *Institutes of Biblical Law,* 182–85).

34. Patrick Deneen, "Abandoning Defensive Crouch Conservatism," *Postliberal Order,* Nov. 17, 2021.

35. Quoted in Julie J. Ingersoll, *Building God's Kingdom: Inside the World of Christian Reconstruction* (New York: Oxford University Press, 2015), 221–23.

36. Ibid.

37. Jonathan Eig, *King: A Life* (New York: Farrar, Straus and Giroux, 2023), 360.

6: The Rebellion

1. Glenn Ellmers, "'Conservatism' Is No Longer Enough," *American Mind,* March 23, 2021, https://americanmind.org/salvo/why-the-claremont-institute-is-not-conservative-and-you-shouldnt-be-either/; Adrian Vermeule, "Integration from Within," *American Affairs* 2, no. 1 (Spring 2018), https://americanaffairsjournal.org.

2. Ellmers, "'Conservatism' Is No Longer Enough"; Glenn Ellmers, "Hard Truths and Radical Possibilities," *American Greatness,* Nov. 23, 2022; https://amgreatness.com.

3. Patrick J. Deneen, *Regime Change: Toward a Postliberal Future* (New York: Sentinel, 2023), 152, 181–82, 184.

4. Ibid., 152; Ellmers, "'Conservatism' Is No Longer Enough."

5. Vermeule, "Integration from Within"; Adrian Vermeule, "Beyond Originalism," *Atlantic,* March 31, 2020, https://www.theatlantic.com.

7: Trump, Savior and Destroyer

1. Michael C. Bender, *"Frankly, We Did Win This Election": The Inside Story of How Trump Lost* (New York: Hachette, 2021), 25–26.

2. Among those who earned less than $50,000 a year, 51 percent voted for Clinton and 41 percent voted for Trump. Among those who earned between $50,000 and $74,900 a year, 48 percent voted for Clinton versus 46 percent for Trump. But of those earning between $100,000 and $199,999 a year—the upper middle class—Trump beat Clinton 49 to 48 percent, and among the highest earners, those making more than $250,000, Trump and Clinton split the vote, 46 to 46 percent. The one group that went overwhelmingly for Trump was those earning between $75,000 and $99,999. Among these solidly middle-class voters (the median middle-class income in 2016 was $78,442), Trump beat Clinton by 16 points, 55 to 36 ("2016 and 2018 Voter Demographics, Based on Validated Voters," *Pew Center Report*, Sept. 8, 2020, https://docs.google.com/spreadsheets/d/1dh8w8Osyc7ZfRC2EsgehTVTV1DOolhFxGgyI_oRfFxM/edit#gid=0; "Exit Polls 2016," CNN, accessed Nov. 10, 2023, https://edition.cnn.com/election/2016/results/exit-polls/national/president).

3. In 2008, with white people making up 74 percent of the vote, McCain won by 12 points over Obama while getting 31 percent of the Hispanic vote and 35 percent of the Asian vote. In 2012, the Republican percentages among Hispanics and Asians dropped to 27 and 26, respectively—thanks, no doubt, in part to Romney's stauncher stance against immigration ("How Groups Voted in 2000," "How Groups Voted in 2004," "How Groups Voted in 2008," "How Groups Voted in 2012," "How Groups Voted in 2016," "How Groups Voted in 2020," Roper Center, https://ropercenter.cornell.edu).

4. The suggestion by some that part of the Republican turn toward Trump was driven by disillusionment with the Iraq War is not well supported. Polls show that a majority of Republicans, unlike Democrats, consistently through the 2000s and into the 2010s, believed the United States made the "right" decision in using military force in Iraq. In 2018, 61 percent of Republicans polled agreed that it was the

"right" decision, as opposed to 27 percent of Democrats. Conservative Republicans, moreover, were even more favorable than moderate Republicans. Trump may have decided to repudiate his own earlier position on Iraq in order to attack the Republican establishment, but, remarkably, most conservative Republicans continued to defend the decision when asked by pollsters (J. Baxter Oliphant, "The Iraq War Continues to Divide the U.S. Public, 15 Years After It Began," Pew Research Center, March 2018, https://www.pewresearch.org).

5. Quoted in Matthew Continetti, *The Right: The Hundred Year War for American Conservatism* (New York: Basic Books, 2022), 383.

6. Michael C. Bender, "To Trump's Hard-Core Supporters, His Rallies Weren't Politics. They Were Life," *Washington Post,* July 16, 2021.

7. Dan Rosenzweig, "Jan. 6 Shattered Her Family. Now They're Trying to Forgive," *Washington Post,* Sept. 9, 2023, https://www.washingtonpost.com.

8. "Donald Trump told me that we have a voice," the same participant said, "and now I stand up for myself" (quoted in Bender, *"Frankly, We Did Win This Election,"* 2).

9. Robert A. Pape, "What an Analysis of 377 Americans Arrested or Charged in the Capitol Insurrection Tells Us," *Washington Post,* April 6, 2021.

10. Zack Beauchamp, "A New Study Reveals the Real Reason Obama Voters Switched to Trump," *Vox,* Oct. 16, 2018, https://www.vox.com.

11. McKay Coppins, "What Mitt Romney Saw in the Senate," *Atlantic,* Sept. 13, 2023.

12. Adrian Vermeule, "Integration from Within," *American Affairs* 2, no. 1 (Spring 2018).

13. Gordon S. Wood, *The Creation of the American Republic, 1776–1787* (Chapel Hill: University of North Carolina Press, 1969), 285.

14. Max M. Edling, *A Revolution in Favor of Government: Origins of the U.S. Constitution and the Making of the American State* (New York and Oxford, U.K.: Oxford University Press, 2003), 16.

15. James Madison, Virginia Ratifying Convention, June 20, 1788, *Papers of James Madison,* vol. 11, 163.

A NOTE ABOUT THE AUTHOR

Robert Kagan is senior fellow at the Brookings Institution and editor-at-large at *The Washington Post.* He is the author of *The Ghost at the Feast, The Jungle Grows Back, The World America Made, The Return of History and the End of Dreams, Dangerous Nation, Of Paradise and Power,* and *A Twilight Struggle.* He served in the U.S. State Department from 1984 to 1988. He lives in Virginia.

A NOTE ON THE TYPE

This book was set in a modern adaptation of a type designed by the first William Caslon (1692–1766). The Caslon face, an artistic, easily read type, has enjoyed more than two centuries of popularity in the United States. It is of interest to note that the first copies of the Declaration of Independence and the first paper currency distributed to the citizens of the newborn nation were printed in this typeface.

Typeset by Scribe,
Philadelphia, Pennsylvania

Printed and bound by Lakeside Book Company,
Crawfordsville, Indiana

Designed by Michael Collica